CLASSIC AMERICAN
CONVERTIBLES

**BY JAMES M. FLAMMANG
AND THE AUTO EDITORS OF CONSUMER GUIDE®**

Publications International, Ltd.

Louis Weber, C.E.O.
Publications International, Ltd.
7373 North Cicero Avenue
Lincolnwood, Illinois 60646

Permission is never granted for commercial purposes.

Manufactured in USA.

8 7 6 5 4 3 2 1

ISBN: 0-7853-1629-9

Library of Congress Catalog Card Number: 95-72905

PHOTOGRAPHY

The editors gratefully acknowledge the cooperation of the following people who have supplied photography to help make this book possible. They are listed below.

Special thanks to: Larry Gustin & David Roman, **Buick Public Relations;** Brandt Rosenbush, **Chrysler Historical Society;** Helen J. Early, James R. Walkinshaw, **Oldsmobile History Center;** Laura Toole, **Chevrolet Public Relations;** Dan R. Erickson, **Ford Photographic Services;** Christina M. Purcell, **Cadillac Public Relations;** Randy Fox, Dan Green, **Pontiac Public Relations;** C. Thomas.

Front Cover: Dan Lyons
Back Cover: Dan Lyons; Vince Manocchi.

AMC-Milton Gene Kieft; Nicky Wright **AUBURN-CORD-DUESENBERG**-Milton Gene Kieft; Nicky Wright; Bud Jueanu; Vince Manocchi **BUICK**-Nicky Wright; Jay Peck; Bud Juneau; Vince Manocchi; Doug Mitchel; Mike Mueller; Milton Gene Kieft; Chan Bush; Bill Kanz; Sam Griffith; Rick Schick; Scott Baxter; Jim Thompson **CADILLAC**-Vince Manocchi; Milton Gene Kieft; Nicky Wright; Gary Smith; Mike Mueller; Sam Griffith; Doug Mitchel; Bud Juneau; Dan Lyons; Richard Spiegelman **CHEVROLET**-Vince Manocchi; Bud Juneau; Doug Mitchel; Sam Griffith; Milton Gene Kieft; Nicky Wright; Mike Mueller; Rob Van Schaick; Dan Lyons; **CHRYSLER**-Nicky Wright; Chan Bush; Milton Gene Kieft; Vince Manocchi; Doug Mitchel; Bud Juneau; Mike Mueller; Sam Griffith **DESOTO**-Vince Manocchi; Bud Juneau; Joseph H. Wherry; Milton Gene Kieft **DODGE**-Nicky Wright; Doug Mitchel; Milton Gene Kieft; Mike Mueller; Vince Manocchi; S. Scott Hutchinson; Terry Boyce; Bud Juneau; Dan Lyons; Thomas Glatch **EDSEL**-Bud Juneau; Nicky Wright; Dan Lyons; Milton Gene Kieft **FORD**-Thomas Glatch; Nicky Wright; Jerry Heasley; Dan Lyons; Eddie Goldberger; Vince Manocchi; Bud Juneau; Phil Toy; Doug Mitchel; Doug Dalton; Richard Spiegelman; Mike Mueller; Jim Thompson **HUDSON-ESSEX-TERRAPLANE**-Vince Manocchi; Doug Mitchel; Jim Frenak; Bud Juneau; Sam Griffith **KAISER-FRAZER**-William A. Coby; Sam Griffith; Doug Mitchel **LaSALLE**-Bud Juneau **LINCOLN**-Vince Mannochi; Gary Smith; Sam Griffith; Dan Lyons; Milton Gene Kieft; Mike Mueller; Nicky Wright; Steve Statham; Michael Brown; Rob Van Schaick; Bud Juneau **MERCURY**-Bud Juneau; Nicky Wright; Scott Baxter; Vince Manocchi; Milton Gene Kieft; Mike Mueller; Sam Griffith; Mike Hastie; Thomas Glatch **NASH RAMBLER**-Thomas Glatch; Milton Gene Kieft; Nicky Wright; Chan Bush **OLDSMOBILE**-Nicky Wright; Denis L. Tanney; Jim Thompson; Tom Buchkoe; Vince Manocchi; Milton Gene Kieft; Dan Lyons; Tom Shaw; Thomas Glatch; Joe Bohovic; Ken Winter; Gary Greene; Bud Juneau; Steve Statham; Sam Griffith; Jay Peck **ORPHANS & UNDERDOGS**-Miton Gene Kieft; Nicky Wright; Doug Mitchel; Richard Spiegelman; Jeffrey I. Godshall Collection; Dan Stockum; Vince Manocchi **PACKARD**-Dan Lyons; Nicky Wright; Milton Gene Kieft; Doug Mitchel; Bud Juneau; Fergus Hernandes; Gary Smith **PIERCE-ARROW**-Milton Gene Kieft **PLYMOUTH**-Vince Manocchi; Sam Griffith; Dan Lyons; Mike Mueller; Dan Lyons; William J. Schintz; Milton Gene Kieft; Nicky Wright; Doug Mitchel; Alan Hewko; Bob Bohovic; Ron Jautz **PONTIAC**-Sam Griffith; Bud Juneau; Doug Mitchel; Tom Storm; Thomas Glatch; Vince Manocchi; Nicky Wright; Gene's Studio; Richard Spiegelman; Mike Mueller; Dan Lyons **SHELBY**-Mike Mueller; Sam Griffith **STUDEBAKER**-Nicky Wright; David Templ; Vince Manochhi; Dan Lyons; Doug Mitchel; Richard Quinn Collection; Richard Spiegelman

OWNERS

Special thanks to the owners of the cars featured in this book for their enthusiastic cooperation; they are listed below.

Front Cover: Glenn & Barbara Patch
Back Cover: John Kepich; Greg Gustafson; Terry Lucas.

AMC-Karl W. Smith; Lee Pontius **AUBURN-CORD-DUESENBERG**-S. Ray Miller; A.B. Folladou; James N Day; Elwood Greist; Micheal Doyle; Terry Radey; William L. Plunnicett; Walter G. Serviss; Ronald B. Irwin **BUICK**-Robert Zaitlin; Edward L. Goehring; Marshall R. Nelson; Peg & Paul Mather; Terry Johnson; Fraser Dante Limited; Rick Schick; Doug & Sonja Waggoner; Kurt Fredricks; Peter & Jane Schlacter; Blaine Jenkins; Gary L. Walker; John M. Galandax; Paul A. Buscemi; Michael L. Berzenye; Walter J. Smith; Rear Admiral Thomas J. Patterson Jr.; Harold Lee Lockhart; Larry E. Driscoll; Anthony Johnson; Tom West; Steve & Sally Kuss; Junior Markin; Dennis Reboletti; Curtis W. Schuetz; Patricia A. Schelli **CADILLAC**-William Young; Dave Holls; Fran Roxas; William Lyon Collection; Terry Radey; Rod Morris; Dick Pyle; Thomas B. Smiley; Walter E. Herman; Harry Nicks/Nicks Old Car Specialty; Dr. Steven Colsen; F. James Garbe; Myron Reichert; Greg Gustafson; Sheldon Grover; Robert N. Seiple;

Robert & Gene Fattore; Dean Stansfield; Dean J. Moroni; John Gaylord; Ed Oberhaus **CHEVROLET**-Tom Meleo; Chris Lapp; Jim & Mary Ashworth; Bobby Wiggins; Dennis G. Wise; Norman Ploggs; Ray Ostrander; Bill & Rita Malik; Julie M. Braatz; Gary Mills; Terry Lucas; Vivian Riley; Bill Jones; Gary A. Girt; Chuck Henderson; Phillip & Sandy Lopiccolo; Steve Sydell; Jeanne C. Finster; Richard & Joyce Dollmeyer; Rob Embleton; Bill Bush; Marty & Jacque Metzgar; Greg G. Grams/Volo Museum & Auto Sales; James E. Collins; Charley Liddard; Dan & Joyce Lyons; Mark Alter; Jim Miller; Steve Donnell/ Donnell Body Shop; Blaine Jenkins; Chip Werstein; Herbert Zinn; Jackie Peacock; Tom Korbas; Jay T. Nolan **CHRYSLER**-Robert N. Carlson; Harry & Virgina DeMenge; John G. Oliver III; Bob Brannon; Ralph Hartsock; Bob & Roni Sue Shaprio; Richard Carpenter; Ray Shinn; Roy Sklarin; Dick Tarnuter/Wisconsin Dells Auto Museum; Lou Schultz; Bryan McGilvray **DESOTO**-Bruce B. Kennedy; Donald E. Desing; Robert Bradley; Raymond J. Reis; T.L.(Tim) Graves; Jess Ruffalo; Jim Crossen; Jeff & Aleta Wells **DODGE**-S. Ray Miller; Jeff Walther; Bill Bost; Jeff Walther; Stanley & Phyllis Dumes; James Milemak; Harry & Virgina DeMenge; Marvin & Joan Hughes; Maurice B. Hawa; Mervin Afflerback; Paul Garlick; Ward Hartsock; Jim Donaldson; Scott Brubaker; Ray Banuls; Tom Devers; Jeffery Baker **EDSEL**-Andrew Alphonso; Cliff Felpel; Dennis L. Huff; Charlie Wells **FORD**-Richard Bayer; Bob & Karyn Sitter; David Patterson; Louis Grosso; Evan & Dolores Martin; William Lyon Collection; Alan Simpson; S. Ray Miller, Jr.; Fred C. Fischer; Donald Passardi; Jack Buchannan; Charles & Raymond Saathoff; John Baker, Sr.; Jackie & Shana Cerrito; Tom Franks; Edward R. Keshen; Alan Wendland; Gerry Klein; William Amos; William R. Muni; T. Davidson & H. Rothman; Mike Spaziano; Steve Thompson; Kenneth & Linda Coleman; Joseph A. Pessetti; Ken Leaman; Doug & Jimmy Call; Claud E. Daniel; Mike & Marge Tanzer; Daniel H. Mitchell; Vince & Helen Springer; Lawrence Keck; Irene A. Galier; Thomas J. & Kathryn P. Shanley; Michael Baker; Steve Engeman; Doug & Teresa Huidston; Frank Trummer; Gary M. Gunushian; Mitch Lindahl; Charles & Marie Cobb; Leroy Lasiter **HUDSON-ESSEX-TERRAPLANE**-Wayne R. Graefen; Ken Poynter; Jack Miller; Chicago Car Exchange, Inc. **KAISER-FRAZER**-Bill Hubert; Arthur Sabin; Ray Frazier **LaSALLE**-Ed Gunther **LINCOLN**- Jack Passey, Jr.; David Holls; Domino's Classic Cars/Ann Arbor, MI; Jack Bart; Harold Von Brocken; Thomas F. Lerch; Jon Woodhowe; Clayton Nichols; Cal & Nancy Beauregard; Carl & Mary Allen; Roger Clements; John Wood; Blaine Jenkins; Eldon T. Anson; Patricia & Rexford Parker; Greg Grams/Volo Auto Museum/Volo, IL **MERCURY**-Jack Karleskind; Richard Kuhn; Joe & Chris Jelinski; Jerry & Jackie Lew; Gary Richards; Ross Gibaldi; Jim Mueller; J.W. Silveira; Jerry Capizzi; Classic Car Centre; Sam H. Scoles; Bob Sejnost; Robert Dowd; Jim Ashworth; Richard Defendorf; Val Price **NASH RAMBLER**-Douglas A. Ogilvie; John W. Beebe; Dick Tarnutzer/Wisconsin Dells Auto Museum; Vince Ruffolo; Chuck Rizzo; Billy J. Harris; T.L. Ary **OLDSMOBILE**-Dean & Deborah Tuggle; Carlo Cola; Terry Johnson; Glenn D. Kelly; Gerald Quam; Peter's Motorcars/Milan,OH; Deer Park Car Museum/Escondido,CA; Charles H. Jackson; Jim Lahti; Gordon Christl; Ralph R. Leid; Bill Clifford; George Kling; Jim Davidson; Austin W. Fray; Howard Von Pressentin; James R. Suther; Linda L. Naeger; Ron Johnson; Neil & Amber Matranga; Bob Weggenmann; Jim McCann; Fran Muckle; Tom Berthelsen; Fraser Dante Ltd./Roswell, GA **ORPHANS & UNDERDOGS**-Ken Rathke; Alexander Marshall; Ken & Stephanie Dunsire; Bruce McBroom; Dr. Barbara Atwood; Ernest J. Toth Jr. **PACKARD**-Les Bowen; Eric M. Thurstone; Armin F. Mittermaier; Paul Mehes; N. Gene Perkins; Kenneth C. Wessel; George D. Kanaan; Darvin & Becca Kuehl; Ned A Torrence; Chuck Mitchell; Armand A. Annereau, Jr. David Reidy; Dave Holls; John Kepich; Ralph R.C. Geissler; Richard P. Lesson; David Burkholder; M.J. Strumpf **PIERCE-ARROW**-P.Alvin Zamba **PLYMOUTH**-Harry & Virgina DeMenge; Dick Pyle; Myron Davis; Paul Avleinbohm; Mearl Zeigler; Mervin Afflerbach; Jack Driesenga; Keith Thomson; Aaron Kahlenberg; John & Shirlee Rasin; Dick Braun,Classic Car Center; Dave Bartholemew; Mary Lee Cipriano; Robert Beechy; Jim Clark; Richard Carpenter/Yesterday Once More; Joseph J. Eberle; Leon Bosquet **PONTIAC**-Tom Hall; Richard L. Nitz; John Sanders; David L. Stanilla; June Trombley; Jim Milne; John Krempasky; Dick Hoyle; Jerry Cinotti; Danny & Barbara Bales; Melvia Lewis; Wanda Habenicht; Joe Kelly; Chris Hunter; Marvin Friedman/Autoputer, Inc.; Dave & Cindy Keetch; Thomas M. Nicholson; John Slavich; Si Rogers; David Snodgrass; Patrick & Barbara Dugan; Neil Ehresman; Larry Zivek **SHELBY**-Samuel Pampenella, Jr.; Lewis H. Hunter **STUDEBAKER**-Ed Warner; Raymond E. Dade; Burt Van Flue; Michelle D. Myer; David Neiber; M.J. Shelton; Anthony Patane; Doug Moysnik

TABLE OF CONTENTS

Introduction: Romancing the Road 6

American Motors 8

Auburn-Cord-Duesenberg 14

Buick 20

Cadillac 32

Chevrolet 44

Chrysler 58

DeSoto 70

Dodge 78

Edsel 90

Ford 94

Hudson-Essex-Terraplane 108

Kaiser-Frazer 114

LaSalle 118

Lincoln 122

Mercury 132

Nash and Rambler 142

Oldsmobile 148

Packard 160

Pierce-Arrow 168

Plymouth 172

Pontiac 184

Shelby 196

Studebaker 200

Orphans & Underdogs: Crosley, Franklin,
Graham-Paige, Hupmobile, Marmon,
Muntz, Reo, Stutz 208

Index 215

ROMANCING THE ROAD

Convertible. Just say the word aloud, and a wistful grin is likely to decorate the face of anyone who's driven a few of these romantic fantasy machines.

With the top down, convertibles deliver a welcome sensation of freedom, a dose of vitality, an experience of exuberant, all-out fun in the sun. Whether alone or in pleasant company, you're on the road, senses stimulated, savoring the good life with the breeze in your face. Although not the height of practicality in all parts of the country, a convertible turns the most mundane journey—even a daily commute—into a rewarding adventure. All your troubles seem to be left behind. You're aware of the surrounding environment, enjoying an unfettered view in every direction. Not only do you see the world, you hear it, smell it, almost taste it.

Even if the top isn't down at the moment, it's comforting—indeed, viscerally satisfying— to know that it could be. Even when standing still, for that matter, convertibles look compelling, as though they know certain secrets that other automobiles cannot fathom. Although the market share of convertibles has always been modest—never exceeding six percent—they've attracted considerably more attention than their mundane mates. Not without cause have dealers typically stationed a fully loaded convertible in the most prominent spot on showroom floors. A few psychologists in the Fifties even theorized that, in the fevered minds of male car-shoppers, a red ragtop symbolized a mistress. More often than not, a man would drive home a practical sedan or wagon, satisfying the family-focused element of his personality. Thus, suggested the speculative shrinks, he chose love over lust—but with a wistful glance backward at that exotic, dream-inspiring droptop he left behind. In today's far different social climate, of course, both male and female shoppers are likely to be attracted to that convertible in the window, imagining the delights that await.

To qualify as a convertible, a car's top must be permanently attached to framework that folds down, either by hand or with power assistance. The roof itself need not be soft, as witness Ford's retractable hardtop of 1957–59.

A true convertible provides weather protection via roll-up windows, not side curtains. By definition, then, that excludes the roadsters and touring cars that lingered through the mid-Thirties, as well as many imported roadsters that began to arrive Stateside after World War II.

Convertible purists add the proviso that the car must be pillarless: fully open, with no structural member other than the windshield protruding above the beltline. We're not quite that rigorous, so several not-quite-total convertibles appear in these pages. Two-doors dominate the ranks, but some of the most memorable ragtops have had four. With a couple of later exceptions—Kaisers and Frazers of 1949–51, Continental of the Sixties—the convertible sedan disappeared by the time World War II began.

Convertibles first appeared in 1927, issued by at least nine manufacturers: Buick, Cadillac, Chrysler, duPont, LaSalle, Lincoln, Stearns, Whippet, and Willys. Many more joined in 1928. By the Thirties, most automakers were turning out at least one and sometimes several, even during the depths of the Great Depression.

Two-doors typically were called cabriolets; and later, convertible coupes. Hudson named its open two-doors "broughams." Four-doors were generally called convertible sedans, though General Motors preferred "convertible phaetons."

Convertibles sold well as the Depression waned and the economy revived, garnering a 2.7-percent market share in 1941. After World War II, in 1950, no fewer than 33 convertible models were on sale. By then, they had a new rival: the pillarless "hardtop convertible" that blended the airy beauty of a ragtop with the comforts of a closed car.

If the convertible had a "golden age," it has to be the late Fifties and early Sixties. By 1957, most American convertibles were powerful and packed with gadgetry. Automatic transmissions were the rule, two-tone paint enhanced the cars' appeal, and tailfins—well, fins existed to be loathed or admired.

Unlike opulent automobiles of an earlier age, these late-postwar convertibles were affordable. Anyone with a good job could sign on the dotted line and drive a dreamboat home to the suburban carport. More than 300,000 droptops were sold in 1957 alone.

Styling was toned down industry-wide in the early Sixties, though horsepower ratings continued to rise as the muscle-car era arrived and dealers discovered the youth market. Automakers who'd offered a single convertible a decade earlier now had four, six, even eight open models. Industry production peaked at more than half a million ragtops in 1965.

By 1970, though, the love affair was faltering. A few years later, America's "final" convertible would go on sale—the 1976 Cadillac Eldorado, inducing thousands to pay far above sticker price to grab one of the last examples of an extinct breed.

Why the decline? Rising insurance rates and increased governmental regulations played roles, but the main culprit was lack of consumer interest. With air conditioning readily available, no one needed a convertible to survive the hot summer. Sunroofs, moonroofs, and T-tops delivered at least part of the sensation of open-air motoring.

Worse, convertibles were viewed by some as frivolous, and inappropriate to changing times—especially in the wake of the 1973–74 OPEC embargo, which alerted America to the precarious nature of the world's oil supply.

Few imagined that convertibles ever would return. Then, in 1982, Chrysler Corporation chief Lee Iacocca authorized a conversion company to snip the tops off a few thousand front-drive Chrysler LeBarons and Dodge 400s. A new die was cast, as ragtop-starved Americans paid a bonus to get one of the first convertibles off the line. Ford soon followed with the droptop Mustang and GM entered the fray with the Cavalier and Sunbird. Not all have sold strongly, but the LeBaron—restyled in 1987—enjoyed a surprisingly hearty run before being replaced by a new Sebring in 1996.

All told, convertible development from the early days to the present is a lively, breezy story—not unlike the experience of piloting a convertible yourself, out there on the great American highway.

AMERICAN MOTORS

Created in a merger between Nash and Hudson in 1954, American Motors Corporation abandoned convertibles for the remainder of the Fifties, with the exception of the little Metropolitan. (See Nash listing for details.) Then, in 1961, AMC returned to the ragtop fold, launching an open version of the compact Rambler American.

Lesser models made do with a 90-horsepower engine, but convertibles—part of the Custom series—had 125 horses to play with. For 1962, the ragtop moved to a new top-of-the-line 400 series.

An Ambassador series had been available since 1958, and a mid-level Classic since '61. Shapelier, all-new mid-size versions of both debuted for 1963, but neither model included a convertible. Not yet, at any rate. *Motor Trend* awarded "Car of the Year" honors to the entire American Motors line.

AMC had ranked fourth in the industry in 1960, rising to third place the next year. George Romney departed the presidency in 1962, replaced by Roy Abernethy. Abernethy's goal: Rival the Big Three in every sector. In 1963, the company built a record 428,346 cars, including more than 321,000 Classics.

Output of the little American convertible dipped to 4750 cars, then nearly doubled in 1964 as the compact series earned a neatly proportioned redesign on a longer (106-inch) wheelbase.

For 1965, AMC had not one but three convertibles ready for the marketplace. This was the company's most impressive ragtop season, with more than 12,000 sold. A low-budget American started at $2418, the Classic 770 stickered at $2696, and an Ambassador 990 brought $2955—or considerably more, unless the buyer used restraint with option lists.

Convertibles remained in the Rambler American lineup through 1967, adopting bucket seats and a Rogue designation. Even the availability of a 290-cid small-block V-8 failed to help sales, which had topped 2000 in 1966 but couldn't even reach half that number in the model's final season.

Ambassadors, too, hung on into 1967, officially abandoning the Rambler prefix after '65. AMC positioned its biggie against full-size Chevrolets, and in 1965 the Ambassador convertible cost just $12 more than an open Impala. Although Ambassadors sold passably well, convertibles failed to take off. Only 1814 and 1260 were built in 1966 and '67, respectively.

Rambler Classics were transformed into Rebels after 1966. AMC produced 1686 Rebel SST convertibles in 1967, followed by a mere 823 the next year (plus 377 Rebel 550s). From 1969 through the Seventies, not a single AMC product went topless.

Not until the mid-1980s did another ragtop roll onto the scene. This time, it wore a Renault badge, because that French company had gained a controlling interest in AMC. Sales of the Renault-designed, front-drive Alliance were encouraging at first, then sunk way down. Cute but suffering from indifferent workmanship and mechanical ills, convertibles were part of the Alliance picture starting in 1985. In 1987, a GTA version carried a 95-horsepower, 2.0-liter engine. Then Chrysler took over AMC and the Alliance evaporated.

New Rambler American... Smartest, Lowest-Priced Convertible!

All New! A Convertible with Rambler Excellence

AMERICA'S NEWEST, SPORTIEST, LOWEST PRICED!

Why just hope for economy?

Proved Economy King. Rambler American Custom with overdrive beat Falcon, Corvair, all other competition, in 1961's biggest, toughest economy contest. *That's Rambler Excellence.*

Think squeaks are standard equipment?

So quiet, you won't believe it's a convertible. Rambler American is the *only* U.S. compact convertible with rattle-free, all-welded Single-Unit construction. *That's Rambler Excellence.*

Rust busting out all over?

Greatest rust fighter is Rambler's Deep-Dip rustproofing—with entire body immersed right up to the roof in rustproofing compound for longer protection against rust. *That's Rambler Excellence.*

Leaving vacation gear behind?

50% bigger trunk in Rambler American sedans for 1961. Take all your vacation luggage. Convertible has far more luggage space than any other compact convertible. *That's Rambler Excellence.*

Pay $478 less for this convertible

It's true. Rambler American costs at least $478* less than the lowest-priced Ford or Chevy 6-cylinder convertible. Beautiful new styling.

Price comparisons based on manufacturers' suggested factory-delivered prices.

Rambler

World Standard of Compact Car Excellence

1

2

1. Not only did AMC reskin the compact American in 1961, it added a Custom convertible. This '62 Rambler American 400—the new top series—sold for $2344. AMC sold an impressive 13,497 convertibles in 1962, out of 125,679 Americans, even earning a profit for its droptop efforts. The convertible's 195.6-cid six-cylinder engine developed 125 horsepower, versus 90 bhp for basic Americans. **2.** Pricing for the Rambler American 440 convertible, wearing a new vertical-bar grille, stood pat in 1963—but output dwindled dramatically. **3.** AMC's only '63 convertible was the Rambler American 440—the top series, albeit with bench seating. **4.** Full 1964 restyling on a six-inch-longer wheelbase helped Rambler American ragtops enjoy a popularity revival, with 8907 built.

3

4

1

1. After producing only Rambler American convertibles in the early Sixties, AMC added two larger companions for 1965. Each had a distinctive front end. The droptop lineup consisted of (*clockwise from front*) a full-size Ambassador 990 with stacked headlights, the American 440 wearing single headlights, and the mid-size Classic 770 with regular quad headlights. AMC built 12,334 convertibles in all, with Classics accounting for 40 percent of the total. **2.** A 1965 Classic convertible might have a 232-cid six-cylinder engine or a choice of two V-8s: 287-cid with a 198-horsepower rating, or 327-cid and 270 horsepower. Ambassadors stretched to a 116-inch wheelbase, while Classics stuck to a 112-inch span; Americans again measured 106 inches.

2

1

2

3

1. Mildly facelifted for 1966, including fresh fender trim, the Ambassador 990 convertible started at $2968. A new two-barrel version of the 327-cid V-8 made 250 horsepower instead of the four-barrel's 270. Some cars had a four-speed rather than Flash-O-Matic or overdrive. Windblown hair kept some women from fully savoring the allure of a lowered roof. **2.** AMC's trusty 232-cid six powers this '66 Rambler American 440, but at mid-season a 290-cid V-8 could be substituted, and a four-speed installed. Facelifted at front and rear, Americans grew three inches longer. Only 2092 American ragtops rolled off the line, with $2486 stickers. **3.** AMC's four-millionth Rambler happened to be a Rebel SST convertible on a 114-inch wheelbase with a $2872 price. The sharp SST series also included a hardtop. **4.** A '67 Rambler Rebel SST could have a 290-cid V-8 to whip up 200 horses or even a big 343-cid engine, impressively rated as high as 280 bhp.

4

1

2

3

1. Ambassadors adopted a rounder profile for 1967, the final year for a full-size convertible now in the DPL series at $3143. **2.** Six-cylinder power remained standard in the 1967 Rambler Rogue, but an optional V-8 made 200 or 225 bhp. **3.** Production of open 1967 Ambassadors totaled 1260, but ten times as many hardtops went to customers. **4.** In 1985, the Renault Alliance was the cheapest ragtop on the market. Series L (*foreground*) cost $10,295; a DL, $1000 more. **5.** Sun-happy buyers snapped up 7141 open Alliances in their opening season. **6.** Just 2015 Alliance convertibles went on sale in 1986.

4

5

6

AUBURN-
CORD-DUESENBERG

As early as 1928, Auburn offered a "cabriolet" body style in five series, from the price-leading 6-66 at $1295 to the majestic, eight-cylinder 115 series. For $2195, the Series 115 buyer got hydraulic brakes and Bijur pushbutton chassis lubrication. Though never a high-volume seller, Auburn soon captured a sizable share of the convertible market. Nineteen twenty-eight also brought the superlative Duesenberg Model J.

All 1928–36 Duesenbergs wore custom bodies, built by such expert coachbuilders as Murphy, Rollston, and LaGrande. The Indiana Duesie factory issued only bare chassis. But what a chassis that was, containing a 420-cid Lycoming straight eight engine, which some observers likened to that of a locomotive. In its original form, the dual-overhead-cam powerplant developed 265 horsepower, shocking for the day. Later came a handful of supercharged examples, dubbed SJ and SSJ, which upped the ante to 320 horses.

Rounding out this trio of full-bore classics was the L-29 Cord, named for company president Errett Lobban (E. L.) Cord. A onetime super-salesman for Moon motorcar, Cord became president of Auburn in 1926. By 1930, his blossoming empire included Duesenberg, the Lycoming engine company, and several other suppliers.

Attempting to fill the broad gap between Auburn and Duesenberg, the L-29 Cord was one of the first production automobiles to employ front-wheel drive—a system developed by Harry Miller, a designer of Indianapolis racers. Styling was by Alan Leamy.

A treat for the eyes, especially in cabriolet form, Cords lagged a bit in the performance department, as they were propelled by a mannerly but modest 115-horsepower Auburn straight eight engine. The L-29 failed to catch on and lasted only into 1931.

Duesenbergs continued to trickle into the market—a mere 470 Model J chassis for the entire 1928–36 period. Auburn introduced a Twelve in 1932; it was the lowest-priced V-12 on the market, with statuesque and imposing bodies atop a 133-inch wheelbase. Rumble-seat cabriolet coupes remained in the Auburn catalog from 1931 through the make's demise in 1936. Semi-streamlined styling for 1934 replaced the prior squared-up profile—culminating in the exquisite Speedster of 1935–36.

By 1936, too, the company was ready with yet another Cord—destined to become one of the most recognizable classics in the world. Again front-drive, the 810 Cord was more compact and maneuverable than its L-29 predecessor, and its 115-horsepower Lycoming V-8 engine produced more satisfying action. Designer Gordon Buehrig penned this Cord, notable for its "coffin-nose" hood and concealed headlights.

Renamed 812 for 1937, Cords could even get a supercharger good for 170 horsepower, enough to turn the 812 into one of the quickest cars on the road. In both 1936 and '37, a pair of two-door convertibles went on sale: a Sportsman cabriolet and a four-window phaeton. After the final Cords went to dealers, the company that had produced some of the most elegant motorcars of all time fell into financial disarray and was dissolved.

A Champion Never Pushes People Around

Any driver that passes the Super-Charged Cord *knows* he does so only with the Cord driver's permission.

The Cord owner has no inferior-car-complex. He does not have to show off, as a sop to his vanity. He is secure in the satisfaction of driving the King of the Highway—capable, when occasion demands, of showing that "thoroughbred" means as much in motor cars as in horses.

The driver of *no other car* is enjoying the same kind of motoring luxury the Cord owner enjoys. Such as easy steering, due to the application of power to the front wheels; a quietness so unusual you can hardly tell whether the engine is running; and a bounceless-swayless-smoothness that can be compared only to coasting.

Besides, the Cord is the smartest car on the road. And, those glistening chrome exhaust pipes on both sides of the hood are not only eloquent signs of greater power and smoothness, but the coat of arms of motoring royalty!

CORD

$1995 *and up, at factory. Freight, tax and equipment to be added*
Auburn Automobile Company, Connersville, Indiana

1

2

3

1. Few motorcars ever approached Duesenberg in elegance. This 1929 Model J convertible, bodied by Murphy, is just one example of that high standard. Its chassis alone, on a 142.5-inch wheelbase, cost $8500. Customers could get an in-house body or order coachwork costing far more. "It's a Duesy" soon entered the language, signifying an item of great worth. 2. A pioneer in front-wheel drive, the Cord L-29 lineup included a convertible coupe from the start. 3. Celebrities of both great- and ill-repute favored Duesenbergs. This Murphy-bodied 1930 convertible coupe was once owned by Al Capone's lawyer. 4. Murphy crafted the rakish Berline coachwork for this 1930 Duesenberg Model J convertible sedan.

4

1

2

3

4

1. Slashing prices in 1931 couldn't keep the Cord L-29 alive. This cabriolet cost only $2495. Just 1433 Cords were built that season, with cabriolet and phaetons the most spectacular. The transmission and final-drive sat ahead of the 298.6-cid straight eight engine. **2.** Even an L-29 Cord's soft top looked large and lumpy when folded. This 1931 convertible phaeton sedan sold for $2595. **3.** Bright paint enhanced the allure of a 1933 Auburn Salon Twelve phaeton, while its 160-horsepower, 392-cid V-12 engine drove a Columbia two-speed axle. **4.** Imposing is the word for a 1932 Auburn Custom Dual Ratio phaeton, with V-12 engine—one of six body styles.

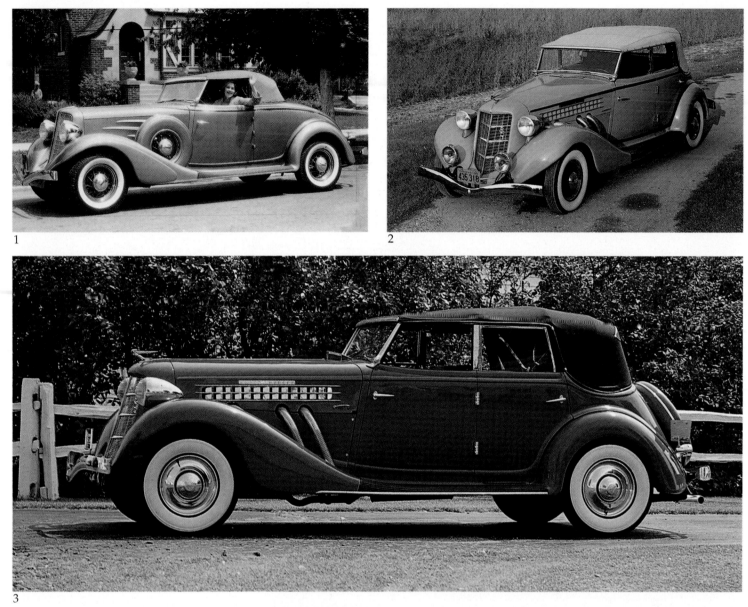

1

2

3

1. Semi-streamlining gave the 1934 Auburn Eight a fresh profile. Cabriolets came in five series, with six, eight, or twelve cylinders, priced from $795 to $1495. Note the triple-hinged "suicide" door. 2. Numbers in the grille identified the 1935 Auburn 851 phaeton, but that body style was offered in four series—Eight, Custom Eight, Salon Eight, and Supercharged Eight. Auburn was sinking financially, but many stronger automakers had fewer model choices. 3. Few 1936 cars looked anywhere near as luscious as an Auburn 852 phaeton. Note the outside exhaust pipes. 4. Even the front bumper of a 1936 Auburn 852 cabriolet coupe flaunted an exquisite curvature. Throughout the early Thirties, Auburns were handsome, quick, and fairly priced—yet the make expired after 1936.

4

1

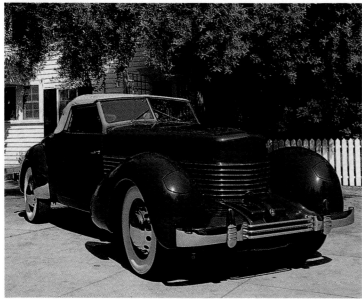

2

3

1. Probably the most recognizable classic of all time, the graceful "thoroughbred" 1937 Cord 812 Sportsman cabriolet designed by Gordon Buehrig featured a "coffin-nose" front end with wraparound louvers, hidden headlights, and full wheel covers. With the optional supercharger—helped by outside exhaust pipes—its Lycoming V-8 developed no less than 170 horsepower. **2.** A 1936 Cord 810 cabriolet could be driven home for $2145. A preselector controlled the four-speed gearbox. **3.** A Cord 810 phaeton cost $50 more than the cabriolet. Both were two-doors.

BUICK

Buick was among the first to adopt the convertible body style, in 1927, with the $1925 Master Six convertible coupe. Renamed the Country Club Coupe for 1928, the soft-topped two-door coupe seated five—a configuration that eventually would dominate the open-car market.

Throughout the Thirties, Buick developed into GM's convertible leader. In 1933, three of the four Buick series included a convertible coupe and four-door "convertible phaeton." A year later, even the posh Series 90 came in soft-top form.

For 1936 Buicks got names instead of numbers. The Special and Century series included convertible coupes, while a Roadmaster phaeton might tempt buyers with more bucks. That four-door body style was available even in the two junior series for '37, but most Buick convertibles sold during this era were Special and Century coupes.

Buick issued phaetons in five levels for 1940—from the $1355 Special to a plush Limited at $1952; convertible coupes came four ways. Buick's final phaetons were built in 1941, and in the Super and Roadmaster series only. By now, Buick was the top builder of convertibles, producing 18,569 two-door models in three series.

No Special or Century convertibles appeared immediately after World War II, but the Super and Roadmaster carried on Buick's eminence. More than 40,000 were built in 1947 alone. By 1951, all three series—Special, Super, Roadmaster—included a droptop.

Introduction of the Riviera "hardtop convertible" in 1949 began to eat into sales of true ragtops. Then, in the early Fifties, Buick's open-car production fell behind that of Ford and Chevrolet.

To energize its image, Buick needed a superstar—and got it with the limited-production 1953 Skylark. Only 1690 were produced, but the rakish $5000 ragtop—sporting notched bodysides and full wheel openings over wire wheels—captured the heart of many a buyer of more mundane Buicks.

Revival of the hot Century as part of a linewide 1954 restyling gave Buick *five* convertibles (including Skylarks). Further into the Fifties, ragtops came in four series, including an ultra-luxury Limited in 1958—a year remembered as Buick's most garish.

Buick's models were toned down stylistically and renamed for 1959. Convertible choices included LeSabre, Invicta, and Electra 225. A compact Special series joined Buick in 1961, with convertibles added the next year—regular Special and fancier Skylark.

Big Buick convertibles remained available through the 1960s—including the Wildcat that was added in '63. Compacts, however, drew more and more attention, especially when Gran Sport editions with potent V-8 engines debuted. Compact convertibles departed after 1972, with the demise of the Skylark badge, but the biggies carried on a little longer—Centurion through 1973, and the final 5300 LeSabres in 1975.

To the surprise of many, Buick was back with a droptop in the Eighties. Just as Chrysler and Ford turned to revived ragtops, Buick elected to have the roof sheared off a moderate number of its ritzy Rivieras. Just under 3900 were built from 1982–85.

Even that wasn't the finale. A two-seat Reatta debuted in 1989, adding a convertible for 1990. Unfortunately, Reattas failed to lure buyers, so Buick's last ragtop to date disappeared after '91.

Shown here is the Buick SPECIAL Convertible, with a dazzling 188-hp V8 engine, and a price that puts this big beauty just a whisper away from similar models of the "low-price three."

It's got Glamor —
and getaway plus

The first part you can judge by eye. Take in the sweep of line, the bold greeting of the Wide-Screen Grille, the smart rake of the rear light assembly—and you begin to see why Buick for '55 is far more than a modest success.

But the next part—the pulse-quickening performance that is putting Buick way up to a new level of popularity—that's something you can judge only by what you feel at the wheel.

When we tell you that every 1955 Buick is boosted to the highest horsepower, Series for Series, in all Buick history, we're just giving you the facts from the record book.

And when we tell you that this rich and spectacular horsepower is now coupled to a new kind of Dynaflow* that, for the first time, brings to the automobile the principle of the modern airplane's variable pitch propeller — we're still giving you the simple facts.

It's what this combination does for you— in getaway, in emergency acceleration, in gas-mileage betterment, and in the sheer thrill of driving—that no mere listing of facts can explain.

It's instantaneous response on getaway. It's absolute smoothness through every single speed range. It's far greater gas mileage in all normal cruising and driving. It's electrifying safety-surge for sudden acceleration to get out of a tight spot on the highway. It's a supreme thrill, and a joy, and a blessing.

We'll be happy and proud to have you try a new Buick with Variable Pitch Dynaflow — and you'll be in for a wonderful new excitement. Come in this week.

Dynaflow Drive is standard on Roadmaster, optional at extra cost on other Series.

MILTON BERLE STARS FOR BUICK
See the Buick-Berle Show Alternate Tuesday Evenings

TOPS IN COLOR — NO EXTRA COST
Every 1955 Buick Convertible is available in any one of the five different top colors shown.

Thrill of the year is Buick

When better automobiles are built Buick will build them

SEE YOUR BUICK DEALER

21

1. By 1935, convertibles had been part of Buick's line for eight seasons. Buick called its open Series 60 four-door a "convertible phaeton." Only 308 were built, priced at $1675, powered by a 100-bhp straight eight. Note the big Trippe lights. 2. Just $1495 bought a 1935 Model 66C convertible coupe with rumble seat, but only 111 customers drove one home. Each Buick series had a convertible coupe. 3. Buick continued its open-car leadership in 1937, offering the convertible phaeton as a Roadmaster (shown) as well as a Special and Century. The Roadmaster's 320-cid straight eight made 130 horsepower. Sidemounts were standard. 4. Even Buick's modestly-priced Special series included a convertible coupe in 1939, priced at $1077 with a 248-cid straight eight.

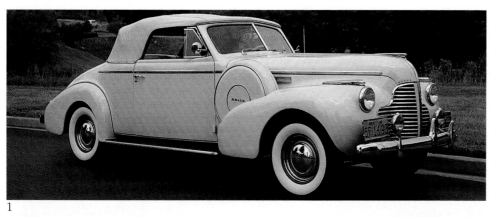

1. Available since 1936, the Century blended a lightweight body with the biggest Buick engine. Sales of the '40 Century convertible coupe were sluggish, partly because Buick revived a stunning Super that year. Note the rare covered sidemount tire. 2. Others had abandoned open four-doors, but Buick still had two convertible phaetons in 1941: the Roadmaster (shown) and a less-costly Super. With new Compound Carburetion, the top engine made 165 horsepower. 3. Fully restyled for '42, Roadmaster bodies were longer, lower, and wider, with "flow-through" front fenders.
4. Except for a modified grille and "bombsight" hood ornament, the 1947 Roadmaster looked similar to '42 models. Buick issued 12,074 open versions.

1

2

3

4

This page: **1.** Buick continued its leadership in convertibles, issuing 11,503 Roadmasters in 1948, plus 19,017 Supers. Roadmasters could get Dynaflow—the first torque-converter transmission. **2.** Three ventiports decorated the 1949 Super, now available with Dynaflow. Automatic transmissions increased the number of women willing to drive the family car. **3.** Starting in '49, Roadmaster convertibles had to compete for sales with the new Riviera hardtop coupe. **4.** This 1950 Super convertible held a 263-cid straight eight. Buick built 12,259 open Supers and nearly 3000 Roadmasters. *Opposite page:* **1.** This $2728 Super was one of three '51 Buick convertibles and the top seller by far. **2.** For 1953, both the Super (shown) and Roadmaster had a new 322-cid V-8 engine, while Special convertibles stuck with a straight eight.

1

2

1

2

1. A dramatically lowered beltline and chopped windshield helped the 1953 Skylark tempt shoppers. The most successful of GM's limited-production ragtops, Skylarks were loaded with accessories and lacked the usual ventiports. 2. In its second (1954) season, Skylark had a gaudier look and lower price, but only half as many were sold. 3. Wire wheels cost extra on a 1954 Super—one of five Buick droptops, including the revived Century. 4. Like its prewar ancestor, the '55 Century tucked a big Roadmaster engine into a light Special body, turning the family cruiser into a virtual hot rod—helped by new variable-pitch Dynaflow. Note the Skylark wire wheels.
5. Buick's lowest-priced 1955 convertible, the Special, started at $2590. Its 264-cid V-8 made 188 bhp whereas other Buick engines measured 322 cubic inches and unleashed 236 horses.

3

4

5

2

1

1. Not too many 1956 Roadmaster ragtops had wire wheels and a continental spare tire, but colorful two-tone paint jobs were common. Buick's 322-cid V-8 yielded 255 horsepower, but had to pull 4395 pounds. **2.** Weakest seller of the four Buick convertibles in 1957 was the $3981 Super, with a 300-horsepower, 364-cid V-8. Not everyone praised that year's facelift. **3.** Stylists ladled on the chrome for 1958, and Buick extended the rear deck of a Roadmaster to create a Limited series, including this $5125 convertible.

3

BUICK

1. Still dazzling but smoother in body contours, Buicks earned angled fins and new model names for 1959. Electra 225 topped the line. 2. A 1960 Electra 225 convertible stickered at $4192, weighed 4571 pounds—and 6746 buyers got one. Buick again had ragtops in three series, cementing its long-standing reputation as an open-roof leader. 3. LeSabre was Buick's least-costly and best-selling convertible in 1960, with a $3145 price and 364-cid V-8. Output totaled 13,588 cars—better than Invicta and Electra combined.

1

2

3

4

5

6

1. After dropping all the way down to ninth in the industry in 1960, Buick reworked its lineup for '61. In addition to launching the compact Special, stylists created an all-new body for full-size models, including this fender-skirted $3382 LeSabre convertible. Canted headlights and "Delta Wing" fins were gone, making the latest Buicks a lot better-looking. The 364-cid V-8 developed 235 or 250 bhp, and 11,951 ragtops went to dealers. 2. Plush 1962 Electra 225 convertibles attracted 7894 customers, despite a hefty $4366 sticker. Buick's 401-cid V-8 made 325 horsepower—necessary to propel nearly two tons of lavish droptop. 3. Compact convertibles arrived for 1962. This Skylark has the 215-cid aluminum-block V-8, rated at 190 horsepower, but less-lavish Special droptops ran with V-6 engines. More than 8900 open Skylarks went on sale, at $3012. 4. Every 1964 Buick series included a convertible, topped by the full-size Electra 225 with its 401- or 425-cid V-8 engine choices. 5. Close to 10,000 LeSabre convertibles rolled off the line for 1963, stickered at $3339. 6. Mildly facelifted for 1964, the Wildcat had debuted during 1962 as a hardtop-coupe variant of the Invicta with a 401-cid V-8. Convertibles arrived in '63, and this year brought the option of a potent 425-cid V-8 rated at 340 or 360 horsepower.

1

2

3

4

1. For 1965, Wildcats came in four body styles and three trim levels. New bodies had a more rounded look, moving to the Electra 225's longer wheelbase. A Custom convertible went for $3727, while the Deluxe brought $3502. Buick issued 9014 open Wildcats—more than 42,000 convertibles in all. This loaded Wildcat has a dual-quad 425-cid V-8. **2.** For 1965, Buick offered a pair of Skylark convertibles—base model and Gran Sport—with an optional 300-cid V-8 that made 210 or 250 bhp. **3.** As usual, all 1966 series except the Riviera included a convertible. This Wildcat has the standard 325-horsepower 401-cid V-8, but Gran Sport editions carried 425-cid engines. **4.** Convertibles still were featured across the 1970 lineup, including this $3700 LeSabre. **5.** Buyers of a 1969 Skylark GS 400 got a lavish dose of "go" along with eye appeal, as a 400-cid Stage 1 engine throbbed beneath the hood.

5

1

2

3

1. Into the Seventies, Buick flashed a flock of ragtops at potential customers. Open Electras departed after 1970, but this 1972 Centurion with a 455-cid V-8 lured 2396 shoppers. LeSabre and Skylark accounted for nearly 6500 more ragtops. **2.** Last of the big open Buicks was the 1975 LeSabre, priced at $5133. This one has the standard 350-cid V-8, but a 455-cid engine was available. **3.** Soon after Chrysler revived a convertible in 1982, Buick skinned the top off some of its sharp Riviera coupes. Open Rivs weren't cheap: This '83 ran $24,950, versus $15,238 for a coupe. Only 1750 were made, but other model years in the 1982–85 period saw even fewer. **4.** For its final stab to date at a convertible, Buick issued an open version of the 1990–91 two-seat Reatta.

4

CADILLAC

In its heyday, Cadillac was the car to which Americans aspired—
the one they'd buy as soon as they "made it." Lush Caddy convertibles, in particular,
captured many a heart.

Cadillac entered the convertible race early, with a rumble-seat model that appeared in
1927. Into the Thirties, the basic eight-cylinder line always included a convertible coupe.
Starting in 1930, 12-cylinder convertibles also turned up, joined by the occasional
mammoth V-16.

Most bodies were created in-house, by Fisher and Fleetwood, rather than ordered from
outside coachbuilders. Cadillac eased into streamlined shapes by 1932–33, and by 1934
Cadillac offered lavish and lengthy convertible sedans, as well as two-door coupes.

Twelve-cylinder models disappeared after 1937, though a second-series V-16 hung on as
late as 1940. In that year, a Series 62 convertible sedan cost $2195, the convertible coupe
$400 less. Their Series 75 equivalents went for $3945 and $3380, respectively, while a V-16
convertible sedan commanded an even $6000. Just two of those were built.

Only Series 62 convertibles remained in 1941, but production reached far beyond prior
years, as 3100 two-doors and 400 four-doors rolled into dealerships.

Convertible sedans departed for '42, as Cadillac adopted a modern profile that continued
after the war ended. In 1947 alone, 6755 customers drove home in a Series 62 convertible.
The next year brought Cadillac's first tailfins, followed in '49 by a new overhead-valve V-8
engine that helped shape the trend toward performance in the Fifties. Before long,
Cadillacs even sported dual exhaust outlets, built into the bumper. References to the new
Coupe de Ville hardtop turned up in song and story, but countless Americans still coveted
one of those finned Caddy convertibles.

GM's Motorama show previewed the 1953 Eldorado, destined to tempt yet another
generation of droptop devotees. Not many people could pay $7750 that year, but the Eldo
soon became a regular in Cadillac's lineup.

Tailfins peaked in 1959 on the Cadillac that, years later, got its rear-end pictured on a
postage stamp—the prime example of Fifties design, if not excess. Fins were gone by '65,
though their vestiges remained on Cadillac bodies for years afterward. Engines grew—429
cubic inches in 1964, 472 in '68, 500 inches for '70. Both DeVille and Eldorado ragtops
attracted customers through the early Sixties, until Eldo went front-drive for '67. By 1971,
the DeVille version was gone but the newly-swollen Eldo was Cadillac's sole convertible.
In a flurry of publicity, Cadillac issued the final Eldorado convertibles for 1976—14,000 of
them, to be exact. Six years later, some owners grew angry—even turning to lawsuits—
when Cadillac launched another convertible. They insisted that Cadillac had promised the
'76 would be its last one. In any case, the $32,000-plus Eldorado Biarritz lasted only two
years (1984–85), ranking as the most expensive convertible in the U.S.

Two seasons later, in 1987, Cadillac had one more convertible ready for the marketplace.
Styled by Pininfarina in Italy, the tasteful and costly Allanté rode a shortened Eldorado
chassis and carried a transverse V-8 engine up front. Sales never reached expectations,
even after an innovative Northstar engine was installed, and the Allanté was dropped
after '93.

Determination has its rewards.

A tradition of building great cars like the 1933 Cadillac 355 Phaeton has its advantages—and rewards—for today's luxury car buyer. First, we stubbornly maintain that a luxury car should be a thing of beauty. This is reflected in all nine Cadillacs—including Eldorado, the only American-built luxury convertible. Then, there's Total Cadillac Value. Because of it, Cadillac resale is traditionally the highest of any U.S. luxury car make...and its repeat ownership the greatest of any U.S. car make. Cadillac. **Then and Now...an American Standard for the World.**

Cadillac '75

GM
MARK OF EXCELLENCE

Cadillac Motor Car Division

CADILLAC

1. By 1930, convertibles were regular parts of a Cadillac lineup that boasted synchro-mesh gearboxes. Top news was the arrival of a 452-cid overhead-valve V-16 engine, as installed in this convertible coupe with Fleetwood body. Its 165-horsepower rating was second only to Duesenberg's. **2.** Cadillac issued 2693 cars with V-8 engines in 1932, including this Model 355B convertible coupe. It was priced at $2945 and weighed 4675 pounds. **3.** Inside, a '32 Cadillac V-8 sported handsome, separate round gauges in a lush instrument panel. **4.** Cadillacs looked more streamlined in 1933, with flowing, skirted fenders. Like other V-16 models, this rare, special-ordered convertible Victoria rode a 149-inch wheelbase and featured an elegant vee'd grille topped by a "goddess" hood ornament. Only two Victorias were built—and a mere 125 Sixteens in all. Ten Fleetwood body styles ranged from $5540 to $8000.

1

2

3

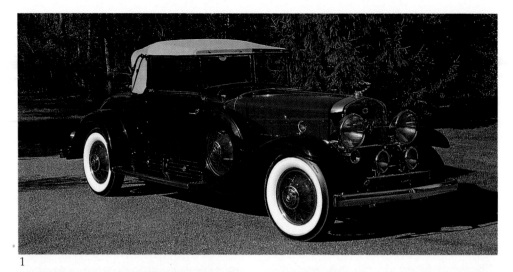

4

1

1. Few could even dream of owning a Cadillac Series 90 V-16 convertible sedan in 1938—not with a $6000 price tag. Just 13 were produced, along with 10 open coupes. Three V-8 series were available, but V-12s were gone. 2. Bohman & Schwartz customized two 1940 Cadillac convertible coupes. Ordinary enough in front but dramatic in profile, each featured notched doors, tilted wind wings, and bucket seats. Workers sectioned several inches out of the car's middle—a technique later used by hot rodders and "homebuilt" customizers. 3. Series 61, Cadillac's lowest-priced line in 1939, included a $1770 convertible coupe. Just 350 were built, with a 346-cid V-8. An open sedan cost $400 more. 4. In 1941, the stunning convertible coupe went for $1645.

2

3

4

1

2

1. Cadillac fielded a convertible sedan for the last time in 1941, part of Series 62, its price cut to $1965. Only 400 went to customers, but that was a lot better than the 75 cars sold in the previous season. Note the stylish fender skirts and single back-up light. Many '41s had the new four-speed Hydra-Matic transmission instead of a three-speed column shift. **2.** Cadillac returned after World War II with a facelift of its '42 models, soon becoming a leader in the postwar ragtop market. Year after year, no other luxury make came close to Cadillac's ragtop volume. **3.** Cadillacs had rounded rear fenders for the last time in '47. The L-head V-8 made 150 horsepower.

3

1

3

2

1. Tailfins first appeared in 1948—quite dashing on this Series 62. Note the tiny back window. **2.** In 1953, Cadillac continued to lead the luxury field in convertibles. A Series 62 droptop started at $4144, with a 210-horsepower V-8 engine. Each of the 8367 ragtops had an automatic transmission. **3.** A new 331-cid overhead-valve V-8 engine, churning out 160 horsepower, went into 1949 Cadillacs, including the Series 62 convertible. **4.** Just 532 fortunate folks drove home a beautifully styled 1953 Eldorado convertible, no doubt because the price was $7750. **5.** Pastel hues enhanced the allure of a '53 Eldo, whose top stowed beneath a metal boot.

4

5

1

2

3

1. Its price slashed to $4738, Eldorado production shot up to 2150 cars in 1954, but the top-of-the-line model now differed less from "ordinary" Cadillacs. The 331-cid V-8 developed 230 horsepower. **2.** Cadillac convertibles were at the top of many drivers' "wish lists." At $4448, a total of 8150 Series 62 ragtops went on sale in 1955, far above Lincoln or Packard volume.
3. Eldorados adopted unique "shark-fin" rear fenders for '55, and offered 20 more horsepower than Series 62 partners. Total convertible output reached a record 12,100 cars.

1

2

3

4

1. By 1956, Series 62 convertibles faced competition from the Sedan de Ville as well as the Coupe de Ville. Even so, 8300 were built, starting at $4766. The V-8 grew to 365 cubic inches and 285 horsepower. **2.** A '56 Eldorado Biarritz convertible cost $1790 more than a Series 62, but the buyer got 20 extra horsepower as well as unique styling touches. **3.** Tailfins towered on 1957 Eldorado Biarritz convertibles. Engine ratings kept climbing, too—now 325 horsepower in Eldos, versus 300 for Series 62. **4.** Distinctive bodywork wasn't enough to keep Eldorado Biarritz sales strong in 1958, as the country sank into deep recession. Only 815 Eldos went on sale.

CADILLAC

1. Whether in red or a more somber shade, the tailfins of a 1959 Cadillac Series 62 convertible shot as far skyward as they'd ever reach. More than 11,000 shoppers said "yes" and drove one home, paying no less than $5455 for the privilege.
2. Eldorado Biarritz output also recovered in '59, with 1320 going on sale. **3.** Cadillac began to trim its fins after '59, but engines remained potent: Breathing through triple two-barrel carburetors, the 1960 Eldorado Biarritz's V-8 yielded 345 horses. This was the last appearance of tri-power and of a hard boot. **4.** Though still strong on chrome, Cadillacs displayed a cleaner front end for 1961. That was enough to lure 15,500 buyers into a Series 62 convertible, again priced at $5455. The Eldorado's price dropped by almost a thousand dollars.

1

2

3

4

1

2

3

4

5

1. In 1962, an Eldorado Biarritz convertible cost $6610—just $1022 more than a Series 62. Each had a 325-horsepower V-8. **2.** Tailfins shrunk further for 1962, but Series 62 convertible volume edged up to 16,800 cars. **3.** Engine refinements improved the 1963 Eldorado Biarritz. It was even smoother and quieter than before, and far less gaudy than its Fifties-vintage predecessors. **4.** A 429-cid V-8 went into the 1964 Eldorado Biarritz, as well as Series 62. Total Cadillac ragtop output neared the 20,000 mark. **5.** Renamed DeVille for 1965, the basic Cadillac ragtop exhibited a squared-off profile and lower silhouette, with only a vestige of fins. Total open-car output reached 21,325.

1

2

3

4

1. Convertible fans still favored Cadillacs, as 1966 output topped 21,000—including 2250 Eldorados priced at $6631 each. **2.** Only a DeVille convertible went on sale for 1967, as the Eldorado adopted front-wheel drive, and was offered only as a hardtop. More than 18,000 ragtops went to customers, at $5608. **3.** Eldorados returned to the ragtop fold in 1971, elbowing aside the DeVille. This '72 Eldo went for $7546, with a 500-cid V-8 that worked up 235 "net" horsepower. A metal boot hid the soft top. A new sunroof option for hardtops cut into convertible sales. **4.** Cadillac issued 8950 Eldorado convertibles in 1975, priced at an eye-popping $10,354. The "final" droptop fleet appeared in '76.

1. After seven seasons without a convertible, Cadillac snipped the roof off the 1984 Eldorado—adding a breathtaking $31,286 sticker. Over two seasons, 5600 went on sale. A new E-body for 1986 did not lend itself to convertible conversion. **2.** The conservative-shaped Allanté was styled and built in Italy, with final assembly in Detroit. Priced at $54,000 in '87, it dropped to $51,500 by 1990, when an air bag was installed. **3.** Allanté rivaled the Mercedes-Benz 560SL, but 1991 sales again failed to reach expectations. **4.** For 1993, Allanté gained Cadillac's fabulous new Northstar V-8 engine, but that wasn't sufficient to keep the two-seater alive.

CHEVROLET

Manufacturer of some of the most coveted ragtops of them all, Chevrolet turned to convertibles early on. Mid-year of 1928 brought the company's first—a sports cabriolet with rumble seat. After a season's absence, that alluring body style returned for 1931 and continued into 1934, joined briefly by a convertible sedan and two-door landau phaetons. No convertibles of any kind rolled out in 1935, but the cabriolet reappeared a year later. Truant for yet another season in 1939, the cabriolet turned up again in 1940. Not only did the open two-door look sharp, it managed to outsell Ford's convertible, even though performance from the overhead-valve six couldn't match a V-8.

In 1942, and again after World War II halted, one convertible model went on sale each year. When the first all-new postwar Chevrolets emerged in 1949, a Styleline DeLuxe ragtop made the cut.

The first Corvettes appeared in mid-1953 as roadsters with side curtains, rather than as true convertibles. Not until 1956 did GM's two-seaters get roll-up windows.

Long applauded as reliable family transportation, Chevrolets got a bold makeover for 1955—plus a much-needed V-8 engine. The 265-cid small-block wielded 162 horsepower in basic form, but a Power Pack added extra horses. In no time, Chevy had adopted a spirited personality and consigned its dreary image to the past. To youthful shoppers, a two-toned Bel Air turned into the hottest low-priced car on the market.

The '56 models couldn't quite match 1955 in panache—or in sales totals. Then came the cars that, for many, still serve as the magnum opus of Chevrolet history: the 1957 Bel Airs. A '57 convertible is guaranteed to send shivers down the spine of today's enthusiasts. Bodies grew bigger and heavier for 1958, when Chevrolet launched a pair of surprises: a flashy Impala hardtop and convertible, and a new 348-cid V-8. Bizarre "batwing" fins and cat's-eye taillights gave the '59 models a memorable appearance.

Chevrolet led the pack in convertibles throughout the Sixties, but had plenty of competition by mid-decade from Ford's Mustang. Rear-engined Corvairs doffed their tops in 1962. So did the Chevy II, but only for two seasons. Mid-size Chevelles debuted in 1964, including Malibu and SS ragtops.

Chevrolet responded to the Mustang challenge in 1967 with the Camaro, which came in convertible form. When the second generation arrived during 1970, however, Camaros became hardtop-only.

Although Malibu and Impala convertibles continued through 1972, the heyday of canvas was past. Only the Caprice Classic and the Corvette hung on into 1975.

Late in 1983, GM turned back to convertibles, starting with the subcompact Cavalier. Only 627 were built that year, but production subesequently rose.

An open Corvette arrived in mid-1986, more than a decade after that body style had departed. Model-year 1987 brought the first Camaro convertibles since 1969.

Camaros lost their angular look in a 1993 redesign that included a shapely convertible. A ragtop rendition of the latest Cavalier arrived during 1995. All three open Chevrolets—Cavalier, Camaro, Corvette—continued going strong as 1996 approached.

Chevrolet Bel Air Convertible
with Body by Fisher.

Blue-ribbon beauty

that's stealing the thunder from the high-priced cars!

Wherever outstanding cars are judged . . . for elegance, for comfort, for beauty of line . . . a surprising thing is happening. The spotlight is focusing on the new Chevrolets with body by Fisher.

Surprising—because Chevrolet offers one of America's lowest-priced lines of cars. But not really astonishing when you consider that its team of internationally famous engineers and stylists spent three years creating the 1955 models, and that they had just one goal—to shatter all previous ideas about what a low-priced car could be and do.

The unparalleled manufacturing efficiency of Chevrolet and General Motors provided the *means*—and that's why you have a

low-priced car that looks like a custom creation. That's why you get the thistledown softness of Glide-Ride front suspension—but married to the sports-car stability of outrigger rear springs. That's why you can choose between a hyper-efficient 162-h.p. V8 engine, or two brilliant new 6's. That's why Chevrolet's array of extra-cost options includes every luxury you might want—Power-glide, Overdrive, Power Brakes and Steering, even Air Conditioning on V8 models. And that's why you should try a Chevrolet for the biggest surprise of your motoring life! . . . Chevrolet Division of General Motors, Detroit 2, Michigan

Motoramic **CHEVROLET** *Drive it at your Chevrolet dealer's*

1. Chevrolet's 1931 Independence lineup included a $615 cabriolet with rumble seat. Output totaled 23,077 cars—close to that of the cheaper roadster. Note the foldout wind wings. A convertible sedan had the same 50-horsepower engine. 2. In 1940, after a year's absence, Chevrolet offered a Special DeLuxe cabriolet for $898. Buyers snapped up 11,820, with the 85-bhp "Stovebolt Six" that had been standard since 1937. 3. Not many '41s beat Chevy's Special DeLuxe for good looks, as 15,296 buyers affirmed. 4. Rear quarter windows were added to 1942 ragtops, now in the Fleetmaster series. Note the full load of accessories: skirts, lights, and hood ornament. 5. Dealers could install "Country Club" trim on 1947–48 convertibles, creating a rival to Ford's Sportsman. The wood on this '47 was added later. 6. A Fleetmaster paced the 1948 Indianapolis 500 race.

1

2

3

4

5

6

1

1. Totally restyled with tempting curves for 1949, Chevrolets looked sleeker yet with fitted skirts. Shoppers eager for an all-new body style grabbed no less than 32,392 Styleline DeLuxe convertibles priced at $1857, just $97 more than the old-style '48. 2. Chevy's new Bel Air hardtop got the glory, but the 1950 Styleline DeLuxe convertible—priced $106 higher—still reigned as the make's glamour queen. Bodies earned a light facelift. Note the tiny back window and extra trim. Chevrolets with new Powerglide gained a larger engine. 3. Convertible sales dipped sharply in 1951, despite a slightly sanitized shape that included bulged rear fenders and a simpler grille. 4. Ragtop prices continued to rise and sales to fall. Chevy's sole convertible, the 1952 Styleline DeLuxe cost $2128, but fewer than 12,000 shoppers agreed to pay.

2

3

4

1

2

1. As part of the square-but-shapely 1953 redesign, Bel Air became a four-model series, topped by the sumptuous $2175 convertible. Red/white was a popular choice. **2.** For the first time in ages, Chevrolet had twin convertibles in 1953. This plainer Two-Ten cost $78 less than the Bel Air, but only 5617 went on sale, against 24,047 Bel Airs. Powerglide and stick-shift cars each had the 235.5-cid engine, but horsepower ratings differed: 115 with Powerglide, 108 with manual. **3.** Pastel hues highlighted the clean lines of the touched-up Bel Air, the only Chevy convertible in 1954, available with a 115- or 125-bhp engine. **4.** Analysts were astonished and shoppers enraptured when the "Hot One" debuted for 1955 with an available small-block V-8. Bel Air convertible pricing started at $2206, but plenty of the 41,268 that went out the door were fully loaded and cost more.

3

4

1

2

3

4

1. "The Hot One's Even Hotter," Chevrolet declared of its graceful 1956 models. The basic 265-cid V-8 in a Bel Air put out 162 horsepower, but twin four-barrels boosted output to 225 bhp. 2. When the sharper-angled 1957 Bel Air ragtop debuted, few suspected it would eventually become a virtual "classic." Buyers had eight engine choices, including 265- and 283-cid V-8s. 3. By 1957, the original Corvette's six-cylinder engine was ancient history. With new Ramjet fuel injection, the two-seater's 283-cid V-8 gave 250 or 283 horsepower. 4. A new Impala hardtop and convertible led the 1958 Bel Air pack, sending Chevy upscale. This one has a fuel-injected V-8, but a new big-block 348-cid engine could be installed.

1. Corvettes lost their hood louvers in 1959 but kept the quad headlights installed a year earlier. The sports car's 283-cid V-8 came in a selection of performance flavors—230 to 290 horsepower, with the option of a four-speed. **2.** Branded as excessive today for its wild "batwing" fins and overabundant bulk, the all-new Impala appeared normal enough in 1959. The dramatic convertible cost $2849 with a six or $2967 with the base V-8. **3.** Close to 80,000 ragtop fans chose a 1960 Impala, now looking almost conservative with toned-down fins and a cleaner front end. Extra-cost accessories augmented its charm. **4.** Fins departed as Chevrolets were restyled for '61. Most Impalas had a 283- or 348-cid V-8, but at mid-year Chevy launched the Super Sport option and legendary "409" engine.

1. Except for a new mesh grille, Corvettes showed little change for 1961.
2. Corvette sales set a record in 1962, when 14,531 were built. Each had the new 327-cid V-8. 3. A Nova 400 ragtop was part of the new Chevy II lineup, and was sold only with six-cylinder power. 4. A Super Sport option added $158 to the price of a 1962 Impala. A new 327-cid V-8 made 250 or 300 bhp. 5. Stunningly restyled to Sting Ray shape, 1963 Corvettes came in coupe or convertible form.

1. Chevy convertibles came in three sizes in 1963: full-size Impala V-8 (*foreground*), Chevy II Nova 400, and rear-engined Corvair, the last available in plain or turbocharged Spyder forms. 2. Squared-off corners and sculpted bodysides identified the '64 Impala convertible, also available in SS trim, with six-cylinder or V-8 power. 3. The 1964 Corvair lineup included two Monza ragtops. 4. Corvettes didn't really need an outside exhaust to look assertive in '65. 5. Costliest of the mid-size 1965 Chevelle models, the Malibu SS wore a black-out grille but might have any engine from a six to a 283- or 327-cid V-8.

1

2

3

1. Big Chevrolets, including the Impala SS convertible, gained flowing lines for 1965. Four V-8 engine sizes were available, but the 409 faded at mid-year. **2.** Reshaped a year earlier, 1966 Corvair ragtops came in Monza (shown) or Corsa trim. Volume fell sharply. **3.** Impalas were mildly facelifted for 1966 and could have a six-cylinder engine or a choice of V-8s: 283-, 327-, or 396-cid. **4.** As usual, Chevrolet's only full-size convertible in 1967 was the Impala, in base trim or as an SS with a newly-available 427-cid V-8. **5.** Not long after its debut as a Mustang rival, a 1967 Camaro SS served as pace car for the Indianapolis 500 race.

4

5

1

2

3

1. Instantly popular, the new-for-1967 Camaro came in convertible or hardtop form, with a choice of two six-cylinder engines. Two-thirds of those built held a V-8, with a 325-horsepower 396 the most potent choice. Typical Camaros were loaded with extra-cost equipment. 2. All 1967 Chevelle SS models got an SS 396 designation, as they had in '66, courtesy of the standard 325-bhp 396 Turbo Jet engine or a 350-bhp upgrade. This soft top has a factory tach and heavy-duty SS suspension. Front disc brakes could now be ordered, but SS 396 production—coupe and convertible—dipped to 63,006 units. 3. Many consider the 1967 Corvette— the last of the Sting Rays—the best of the lot. With triple carbs, the 'Vette's 427-cid V-8 yielded 435 horsepower. 4. No longer a separate series in 1968, the Super Sport was a $179 option package for Impalas.

4

1

2

3

1. Quickly dubbed the "Shark," an all-new Corvette debuted for 1968, wearing a Kamm-style rear deck. Convertibles accounted for twice as many sales as coupes, but that ratio soon would change. **2.** Formerly a separate model, in 1969 the Chevelle SS 396 was an option group that included a double-bulge hood and black-out grille. This ragtop wears white-letter tires instead of standard red-line rubber. Stripes and a power top were optional. **3.** This 1969 Impala SS was no tame Chevy, boasting an SS-427 (Z-24) with 427-cid V-8, which added $422 to the base price. **4.** For the last time until the mid-Eighties, a Camaro convertible went on sale. This '69 SS holds a potent 375-bhp, 396-cid V-8.

4

1

2

3

1. Open Corvettes sold less well than coupes in 1970, despite their lower price—a trend destined to grow. America's Sports Car had a choice of five engines, topped by a 425-bhp 454-cid V-8. 2. More than 37,000 Corvettes went to buyers in 1974, but only 5474 were convertibles. The 350-cid V-8 delivered 195 or 250 horses, or a 270-bhp 454 could be installed. This car has the rare Z07 option, with heavy-duty brakes and suspension. 3. Chevy's last big convertible, the 1975 Caprice Classic, had a standard 350-cid V-8. As before, most ragtops went out the door "loaded," selling for well beyond the $5113 sticker. Just 8349 were built. 4. Revived during 1987, the Camaro convertible came in three levels: base, Z28, or IROC-Z (shown).

4

1

1. Chevrolet's subcompact 1987 Cavalier convertible came only in RS trim, with a four-cylinder or V 6 engine. A year later, Cavaliers earned a neatly-rounded facelift, and the ragtop adopted the sporty Z24 designation. 2. By 1993, Corvettes carried a second-generation LT1 5.7-liter V-8 that developed 300 horsepower. Convertibles could have a 40th anniversary option package. No open versions of the super-performance ZR-1 Corvette ever went on sale. 3. Cavaliers grew curvier and more modern in their 1995 restyling. An LS convertible joined the lineup during the model year. 4. A new "3800" V-6, rated at 200 horsepower, went into 1996 Camaros, but the Z28 was V-8 only.

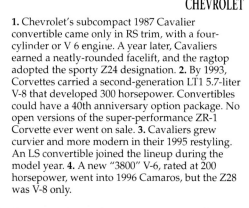

2

3

4

CHRYSLER

No American automaker matches Chrysler's record as a consistent convertible producer. In 1927, just three years after the company's founding, Chrysler introduced its first convertible: a cabriolet in the new Imperial 80 series. A year later, the cabriolet body style switched to the mid-range Model 72's chassis. Well-heeled Imperial customers could order Dietrich and LeBaron custom-bodied convertibles.

From 1931 to 1933, rumble-seated convertible coupes were offered in each of Chrysler's four series. Convertible sedans joined by 1932, led by the lush Imperials.

Radiators tilted back for 1933, a year in which Imperials—their wheelbases as long as 146 inches—again led the pack in style. Chrysler introduced the innovative Airflow in 1934, without open models—and it was difficult to imagine one on its radically streamlined shape. Only six-cylinder Chryslers, then, could have soft tops.

Airstream Chryslers for 1935 might have six or eight cylinders, but convertibles held only a straight eight. A year later, either engine went into open models.

After suffering an ungainly barrellike front end for 1937, body lines smoothed considerably by 1939, but convertibles were omitted. A convertible coupe returned for 1940, but the open sedan was a fading memory.

From 1940 to '42, convertibles came in Windsor Six and New Yorker Eight guise.

After World War II ended, Chrysler had a surprise waiting: a wood-trimmed Town & Country convertible, borrowing a name previously used on a station wagon. Chrysler's last open Town & Country came in 1949, on the well-built but boxy body that served as the company's first truly new postwar car.

Twin convertibles—Windsor and New Yorker—went on sale each year through the early Fifties, accompanied by an open Imperial in '51 only. The first open Chrysler 300 appeared in 1957, two years after that high-performance model had debuted.

Letter-series 300 production slipped in the late Fifties, and New Yorkers weren't selling much better. Meanwhile, in 1957, another Imperial convertible debuted, soon topping Lincoln's sales. Open Imperials were available as late as 1968, employing separate-frame construction until 1967—seven years after other Chryslers had adopted Unibody construction.

Low-line ragtops remained available into the Sixties—Windsor, then Newport. A "standard" 300 series replaced the Windsor in 1962, including a convertible. Newport and 300 convertibles were issued through 1970. Then, ragtops disappeared for a dozen years.

Not long after Lee Iacocca took Chrysler's helm, he ordered the Cars & Concepts company to begin slicing roofs off the new LeBaron (and Dodge 400) coupes, to create the first convertibles of the Eighties. A Town & Country edition arrived in 1983, sporting mock-wood trim. An optional turbocharged engine was added for 1984.

LeBarons earned a shapely restyling for 1987, featuring concealed headlights, as Chrysler led the nation in open-topped motoring. Open LeBarons hung on through 1995, adding V-6 power along the way. Meanwhile, Chrysler's top-down "TC by Maserati" joint venture came and went. Soon after the '96 model year began, Chrysler was ready with yet another convertible—the splashy Sebring.

"TOWN AND COUNTRY"... Chrysler's work-or-play convertible... magnificent in its utterly new styling... magnificent in the smooth, responsive power of Chrysler gyrol Fluid Drive and improved hydraulically operated transmission... another triumph of Chrysler's imaginative engineering—first in the field with the developments that really matter!

the Beautiful Chrysler

FROM COAST TO COAST, SEE A
CHRYSLER-PLYMOUTH DEALER
FOR THE FINEST SERVICE

1. By 1932, when this Imperial went on sale, Chrysler had been issuing convertible coupes for five years. Open coupe bodies went on the long-wheelbase Imperial CL chassis, with a $3295 price, and also were available in Chrysler's lower-cost lines. Note the split windshield, whose panes opened individually to let breezes blow through. **2.** Only 49 Imperial Custom CL convertible sedans were made in 1932, weighing 5125 pounds and priced at $3595. Chrysler's top 385-cid straight eight made 125 horsepower. Non-Imperials also came in convertible sedan form. **3.** Chrysler's lone convertible in 1935 was the Airstream Deluxe Eight, and only 101 went on sale.

1

2

3

4

5

6

1. Few would call Chrysler's 1941 shape breathtaking, but a New Yorker ragtop certainly had appeal. So did its six-cylinder Windsor mate. **2.** Seats and door panels of a '41 could be jazzed up with Highlander plaid or Navajo upholstery. **3.** Fender skirts accented a '42 New Yorker. **4.** Film actor Leo Carillo drew crowds with his customized 1947 Town & Country convertible. **5.** Like many stars, Bob Hope fancied the T&C. **6.** In 1947, a T&C cost $2995. More than 8500 were made from 1946 into '49.

1

2

3

4

1. Though fitted with less real wood than before, and priced higher than most Cadillacs, the 1949 Town & Country attracted a thousand buyers. 2. Nearly 4400 regular 1949 Chrysler ragtops were sold, including 1137 New Yorkers. Windsors accounted for the bulk of sales. 3. A new Hemi V-8, rated at 180 horsepower, powered the 1951 New Yorker, which paced the Indy 500 race. 4. New Yorkers (shown) had a handsome new body in '53. Windsors stuck with six cylinders.

1

1. Lower and sleeker, the "Forward Look" 1955 lineup included a New Yorker Deluxe convertible, its Hemi engine now making 250 horsepower. Lower-priced Windsor ragtops adopted a smaller V-8. 2. Towering fins highlighted 1957 New Yorkers, which gained front torsion bars and a larger engine. Chrysler issued two other ragtops an Imperial and a super 300C—but only 484 of the latter were produced. 3. Just 286 open New Yorkers went to dealers in 1959, each running with a 413-cid V-8. Ragtops also continued in the Windsor and Imperial series. 4. A 1959 Chrysler 300E convertible wasn't cheap at $5749, and only 140 were made, but its snorting 380-bhp V-8 bolstered Chrysler's reputation as a builder of burly machines.

2

3

4

1. Even the big Chrysler New Yorker adopted Unibody construction for 1960, a year in which Chrysler offered four convertibles. AstraDome Instrument panels featured electroluminescent lighting. 2. Fins continued to stretch tall in 1961, and convertible volume rose by nearly 35 percent. This New Yorker stickered at $4592. 3. Never a strong seller, the Imperial Crown convertible coupe fell to 429 units in 1961. Imperials flaunted freestanding headlights for a classic-era image. At $5774, the luxury droptop cost some $300 more than a Series 62 Cadillac. 4. Long, sweeping tailfins added extravagant flair to a 1961 Chrysler 300G, but they'd be sheared off a year later. Only 337 of the high-performance ragtops went on sale, starting at $5841. Their triumphant Ram-Induction V-8 engines liberated as much as 400 horsepower.

1

2

3

4

1

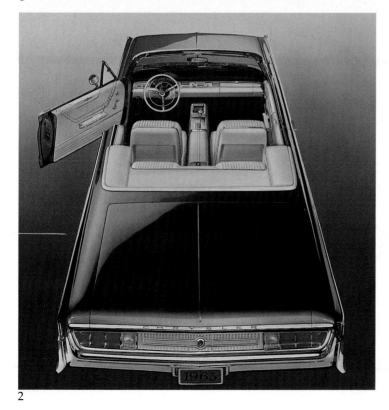

2

3

1. An open Chrysler 300 paced the Indianapolis 500 race in 1963, but it wasn't the fabled "letter series." In fact, the 300J came only as a hardtop. Close to 3400 of the less-costly nonletter 300 convertibles rolled off the line, including 1861 "Pace Setter" models that commanded an extra $339. **2.** For the eleventh time, Chrysler tempted fanciers of big muscle with its legendary supercar. Ending a tradition, the 1965 Chrysler 300L convertible sold for $4618, but only 440 were built—down from a record 625 in '64. Note the long central console between the bucket seats. **3.** Final letter-series Chryslers held a 413-cid V-8 engine, good for 360 horsepower.

1

2

1. Newly Unibodied, the 1967 Imperial began to lose its distinct qualities, becoming more of a glorified Chrysler. A high price ($6244) helped keep output down to a mere 577 ragtops, with a standard 440-cid V-8 that yielded 350 horsepower. 2. Concealed headlights gave the 1968 Chrysler 300 a hint of drama, and its standard 440-cid V-8 was no slouch. Still, the performance pedigree of the 1955–65 letter-series was long gone. A Newport convertible cost $631 less. This year's "Sportsgrain" option emulated the old Town & Country. 3. In high-performance trim, with a 440 TNT engine, a 1969 Chrysler 300 could more than hold its own on the highway. Soft top popularity was sinking, but 1933 were built, many loaded with options.

3

1

1. Chrysler launched the front-drive LeBaron convertible in spring 1982, adding this Town & Country edition with simulated wood in '83. Ragtop-starved fans snapped up the square but sharp LeBarons with a passion. The T&C was no cheapie at $15,595. Upscale Mark Cross LeBarons ran only a thousand less. Convertibles used a Mitsubishi four-cylinder engine. 2. By 1986, all LeBaron engines, including a turbo, were Chrysler-built. Prices ranged from $12,695 to $17,595—a sum that could buy three Ford Escorts. 3. Curvaceously reshaped for 1987 with hidden headlights, a LeBaron paced the Indy 500. 4. Only a Premium LeBaron went on sale at first, with a choice of two engines.

2

3

4

1

3

1. Chrysler began the 1988 model year with base-model and premium LeBaron convertibles. A performance-oriented GTC arrived later, wielding a 174-horsepower, intercooled 2.2-liter turbo and Getrag five-speed gearbox. 2. Chrysler joined forces with Maserati to create the 1989 TC by Maserati. Built in Italy and loaded with extras for its $30,000 price, the two-seater's debut had been long delayed. Either of two turbocharged engines were available. 3. A driver-side air bag went into Chrysler's TC by Maserati for 1990. Fewer than 3000 had been sold in its first model year and 3997 this season, with a few leftovers reserialed as '91 models. 4. By 1990, LeBaron convertibles came in four trim levels with any of four engines, including a Mitsubishi-built 3.0-liter V-6.

4

1. Convertible devotees in 1991 could pay just $15,925 for a LeBaron or $19,175—plus options— for a Premium edition. The GTC, with 174 horsepower, was priced in between. 2. Chrysler not only dropped the LeBaron coupe for 1994, it abandoned lower-priced convertibles, fielding only a GTC. Equipment was added for the '95 finale, without a price boost. 3. For 1996, an all-new Sebring convertible replaced the long-lived LeBaron. Based on Chrysler's Cirrus sedan, the latest droptop holds a four-cylinder or V-6 engine. Note the integrated foglights.

1

2

3

DE SOTO

Starting with just one make in 1924, Chrysler Corporation had four by the end of the decade. In addition to buying Dodge, the company launched both Plymouth and DeSoto. No convertible was included when DeSotos went on the market during 1928, as '29 models. A convertible coupe joined in 1930, in two of DeSoto's three series. That body style sold in modest numbers through 1933, augmented by a convertible sedan in '32. Early DeSotos had six- or eight-cylinder engines, but only sixes continued into 1933. With prices approaching $1000, none of these DeSotos ranked as particularly memorable— though, as usual, open bodies were more striking than their closed counterparts.

In 1934, the only DeSoto to go to market was the radical new Airflow, whose aerodynamic lines and all steel "safety" construction did not lend themselves to an open body style. In fact, it's difficult even to *imagine* an Airflow convertible. A conventionally styled Airstream series joined the Airflow in 1935, including a rumble-seat convertible coupe priced at $835. Only 226 went on sale.

When DeSotos got a restyle for 1936, a $1095 convertible sedan joined the $895 open coupe. Both were part of the Custom Airstream series. Those two body styles continued through 1938, but disappeared in the 1939 season.

Another restyle, this time by Raymond Dietrich, came in 1940, and a convertible coupe made the lineup. Priced at $1095, it sold only 1085 copies, but output rose to a respectable 2937 cars the next year. Just 568 open DeSotos went on sale in '42, selling for $1317 or less.

Convertibles continued in the first three years of the postwar era—based upon the Custom club coupe, again with roll-down quarter windows. Squared-off restyling for 1949 included yet another convertible coupe, again in the upscale Custom series.

Through the Fifties, DeSoto was squeezed between the costlier Chrysler and the cheaper Dodge in its quest for customers—a fate it had endured from the start. Potential convertible sales, meanwhile, were stolen by the new Sportsman hardtop coupe, when it became available in 1950. Two years later, DeSotos could have V-8 engines.

Convertibles came in both series—Firedome and Fireflite—when the flashy '55 DeSotos hit the dealerships. Total output reached 1400 ragtops—well above the usual number. DeSoto issued a hundred replicas of the 1956 Indy pace car convertible, along with 1385 "ordinary" Fireflite ragtops and a fleet of Firedomes.

A limited-production Adventurer series arrived by 1957—hardtop and convertible coupes, flaunting gaudy color combinations and anodized aluminum trim. Only 300 soft-topped Adventurers rolled off the line in 1957, packing a 345-cid V-8 that developed an even 345 horsepower.

All four DeSoto series offered convertibles in 1958 and '59: Firesweep, Firedome, Fireflite, and Adventurer. Production of the limited-edition Adventurer convertible skidded to 82 cars in 1958 and 97 the following year. Total DeSoto output fell 58 percent in the 1958 model year, then further yet.

By the late Fifties, DeSotos cost almost as much as Chrysler Windsors, and their days were numbered. Only closed models went on sale in 1960, and the make expired shortly after the 1961 model year began.

1

1. DeSoto shared its new "steelweld" bodies with Plymouth in 1930. Part of the new "Finer Six" line, the Series CK convertible coupe cost $945, complete with rumble seat and a revised Silver Dome six-cylinder engine that produced 60 horsepower. About 12,200 Finer Sixes were built in 1930–31 but only 184 convertibles—which also came in the CF Eight series. Note this car's landau bars, wire wheels, and sidemounted spare tire. **2.** In 1932, DeSoto issued an SC Custom convertible coupe with rumble seat, priced at $845, plus a pair of lower-priced roadsters and a $975 convertible sedan. Only 960 open coupes were built and 275 four-doors. Bigger and more stylish, the "New Six" models featured a barrel-style grille, new "Floating Power" mounts for the 75-bhp engine and an X-braced chassis.

2

1. Film stars James Stewart and Wendy Barrie posed with a skirted 1936 DeSoto Airstream Custom convertible coupe that cost $895. A convertible sedan brought $200 more, but neither sold in large volume. Airflows hung on, and the Airstream line expanded to include DeLuxe and Custom models. **2.** DeSoto shrunk to a single S3 series for 1937, on a shorter wheelbase. Fewer than a thousand convertible coupes went on sale, at $975, with a smaller six-cylinder engine than in '36. **3.** Likely prospects for convertible sedans were few in number, but DeSoto had revived that body style in 1936. This one cost $1300—hardly small change in '37.

1

2

3

1

1. DeSoto dubbed its reworked 1941 models "Rocket Bodies," insisting that the S8 series was "long, low-slung and rakish." Not everyone concurred in that judgment, but the Custom convertible coupe found 2937 buyers willing to part with $1240. Total DeSoto output soared past the 97,000 mark. Major facelifting included a longer body, lower hood, and bolder front— including the first use of grille "teeth." DeSotos could now have Fluid Drive and Simplimatic, a semi-automatic transmission that reduced the need for gearshifting. Grille guards, spotlights, and foglights were popular add-ons. 2. "Airfoil" hidden headlights made the 1942 DeSoto one of the easiest cars on the road to identify; the lamps were billed as "out of sight, except at night." Convertibles came in both DeLuxe and Custom trim, at $1250 and $1317. DeSoto's six-cylinder engine was bored to 236.6 cubic inches, making 115 horsepower. Running boards were fully concealed behind flared door bottoms, as DeSoto promised "a dream of driving come true."

2

1-2. Like nearly all American automakers, DeSoto resumed production after World War II with mildly modified versions of its '42 models—but in this case, without the short-lived hidden headlights. A convertible coupe was included from 1946 onward. Fenders now reached back into the front doors, and a widened grille retained the vertical bars that had debuted before the war. DeSotos changed little in the first three postwar seasons, so this 1948 Custom convertible coupe, priced at $2296—far above prewar figures—looks much like the 1946–47 models. Fluid Drive with Tip-Toe Shift was installed in top models, and owners could select such accessories as twin spotlights and a grille guard. Desoto's 236.6-cid L-head six developed 109 horsepower. Note the center-mounted stoplight, a hallmark of Chrysler products throughout the Forties.

1. DeSotos adopted a boxy profile in 1949, but a $2578 convertible again made the lineup. This one has a special leatherette interior (normally used in the Suburban sedan). 2. Firedome DeSotos held a 276-cid "Hemi" V-8 engine in 1953, as introduced a year earlier. Just 1700 Firedome convertibles went on sale and none at all in the six-cylinder Powermaster series. 3. "Forward Look" 1955 DeSotos doffed their tops two ways—as a $3151 Fireflite (shown) or $2824 Firedome, the latter with 15 fewer horsepower. 4. Output of the 1956 Fireflite set a record for a single V-8 convertible model, with 1485 built (including 100 Pacesetters). Note the unusual wraparound rear window. By this time, DeSotos wore mesh grilles.

1

2

3

4

1

2

1. Out of four DeSoto series in 1957, three offered a convertible—led by the limited-edition Adventurer, launched a year earlier in hardtop coupe form. At $4242, an Adventurer ragtop was no cheapie. Its dual-quad 345-cid V-8 made one horsepower per cubic inch. Firedome and Fireflite convertibles had a slightly smaller engine. This Adventurer has several extras, including a Highway Hi-Fi record player and a Benrus steering-wheel "watch." DeSotos could be ordered with a PowerFlite or TorqueFlite transmission— both pushbutton-controlled. 2. Only 474 open Fireflites left the plant in 1958, but ragtops came in three other DeSoto series—1775 of them in all. Output dipped below 1200 the next year.

DODGE

Within a year of its 1928 acquisition by Chrysler, Dodge joined the ranks of convertible producers. By 1933, the lineup included a quartet of open models, led by a convertible sedan with six or eight cylinders. Only about 1600 were built.

Eight-cylinder engines retreated into history after 1933, but Dodge continued to issue convertible coupes, and a smaller number of convertible sedans, through 1938. No convertibles made the '39 lineup, but an open coupe returned for 1940. That body style continued through '42 and returned after the war ended.

Dodges got a squared-up restyling in 1949, along with their corporate brethren. In addition to convertibles, Dodge offered something thought to be extinct—a roadster. Wayfarers had side curtains instead of roll-up windows, thus failing to qualify as true convertibles. That deficiency was remedied for 1950 with the short-lived Sportabout. Conventional convertibles in the early Fifties were limited to the premium Coronet series, continuing as Dodge got a revamp and added Red Ram V-8 power for '53. A year later, the model name switched to Royal and 2000 were produced, including 701 Royal 500 Dodges to commemorate the make's duty as an Indy pace car.

A snazzy '55 facelift gave Dodge a fresh stance and a stronger competitive edge. From 1956 to decade's end, convertibles came in two series: Coronet and Custom Royal. "Swept wing" styling with a touch of tailfin marked the '57 Dodges, which gained a D-500 engine option, complete with firmed-up suspension.

Polara and Dart Phoenix models with new unibody construction went to dealers in 1960–61. Then, for '62, full-size Dodges were downsized. Ragtops came in the Dart 440 and Polara 500 series, augmented by a lengthier Custom 880, revived at mid-year.

In 1963, the newly shrunken Dart decided to doff its top, in two trim levels. By 1965, Dodge was issuing seven different convertibles—Polara, Custom 880, a trio of mid-size Coronets, and a pair of Darts—the best ragtop season ever. Then, in 1967, arrived one of the most memorable open Dodges of the muscular Sixties: the 440-cid V-8 Coronet R/T. Five convertibles were available in 1970, in three groups: the new Challenger, mid-size Coronet 500, and full-size Polara. More than 6300 were built, the majority of them Challengers. Only a base-model Challenger convertible hung on into 1971. A Challenger R/T paced the Indy 500, and Dodge prepared 50 replicas. No ragtops at all made the 1972 season.

Not until a decade later, in fact, would any Dodge come topless. Just as Chrysler issued its first LeBaron convertibles during 1982, Dodge did likewise with its 400 series. Converted from coupes, early models weren't terribly well constructed. No matter. Ragtop-happy fans grabbed them anyway. Quarter windows were added in 1984, when production moved to Chrysler's own factory. A turbocharged engine went into the 600 ES, the most collectible of the group.

Chrysler restyled its LeBaron for 1987, but Dodge dealers no longer had a convertible to offer. Not until 1991, at least, when a small number of subcompact Shadows went on sale in convertible form. Those lasted only through 1993. Since then, Dodge has been without any convertible—apart from the "retro" Viper V-10 roadster, which sports removable side curtains instead of roll-up glass.

Let's salvo those convertibles right off the map. You know the kind. The puffed up convertibles with the puffed up price tags. The kind that makes you glad Coronet 500 came along. Coronet's slim and trim. Neat and nifty. Personable. Engagingly attractive. With a big choice of power—from a brisk Six to a go-hummer of a 426 cubic inch Hemi V8. And that's enough to blow most other convertibles right out of the water. But the Coronet 500 convertible, for all that, carries a sweetly reasonable price tag. You don't like convertibles, but want to be in on the Dodge Rebellion? Well, now, we have other Coronets. Sedans, wagons, hardtops, the works. Whichever way you want to sign up, Coronet's really got it. Now at your dependable Dodge Dealer's.

Dodge Coronet

DODGE DIVISION ✦ CHRYSLER MOTORS CORPORATION

JOIN THE DODGE REBELLION

Open fire on ho-hum convertibles.

Open up a Dodge Coronet 500.

LOOK 3-22-66 47

1966

1. All Dodges had six-cylinder engines in 1934, when a convertible coupe cost $765 and a convertible sedan $875. Note the auxiliary trunk—a popular extra. 2. Despite its designation as a "Beauty Winner," the 1936 Dodge came across as more practical than pretty. A sidemounted $2 convertible sedan, on the other hand, exuded enough charm to justify its $995 price—a rather high figure for the day. 3. Convertible coupes still had rumble seats in 1936.

2

3

1

2

3

1. Flirting was a popular pastime, especially from the driver's seat of a convertible—here, a 1938 Dodge D8, complete with rumble seat for $960. A convertible sedan was available for the last time, at $1275; only 132 went on sale. 2. Fender skirts cost extra, and running boards could be installed for the last time on a 1941 Dodge Custom convertible coupe. Dodge's L-head six made 91 horsepower. 3. Soon after World War II ended, Dodge had line-topping convertibles on sale. Inflation pushed prices to $1649 in 1946, then upward to $2189 by '48. 4. Like other automakers, Dodge made do with a mild facelift of '42 models to start the postwar era. Dodge's 230-cid engine was rated at 102 horsepower.

4

1. When it first appeared in 1949, Dodge's Wayfarer ranked as a roadster, with old-time side curtains. For 1950, the Sportabout added roll-up windows, for the same $1727 price. A total of 2903 were built that year, in contrast to only 1800 Coronets. 2. Just over a thousand Wayfarer convertibles were sold in 1951. Note the distinctively curved door-window shape. 3. Dodge touted the ease of operation of a Wayfarer's manual top. 4. Wayfarers seated only three, but a super-long rear deck offered ample luggage space.

1

2

3

1-2. After years of stodgy styling and strictly six-cylinder powertrains, Dodge leaped ahead for 1953 with a shapelier physique and a hot Red Ram V-8 engine that unleashed 140 horses. This Coronet Eight convertible listed for $2494, with 4100 made. **3.** The comedy team of Dean Martin and Jerry Lewis took their act to Indianapolis in 1954, where a Dodge convertible served as Official Pace Car for the prestigious Indy 500 race. **4.** After the '54 event, Dodge issued 701 replicas of the yellow Royal 500 convertible pace car. The $201 option included Kelsey-Hayes wire wheels, a continental spare tire, and performance goodies for the Red Ram V-8. Dealers could even add a four-barrel Offenhauser manifold to the 150-horsepower engine. For the first time, Dodge offered a fully automatic transmission: two-speed PowerFlite.

4

1

2

3

1. "Flair Fashion" restyling for 1955 gave Dodge a longer profile and unique look. The Hemi V-8 in a Custom Royal Lancer—the sole convertible—grew from 241 to 270 cubic inches. Most Custom Royals wore flashy three-tone paint. 2. Dodge fins differed from the pack in 1957, as bodies adopted a still-longer stance. A Coronet convertible (shown) listed for $2842, versus $3146 for the posher Custom Royal. A few cars got the new D-500 option, a 245-horsepower Hemi. 3. Custom Royal Lancers changed only in detail for 1958, but the D-500 option was now a "wedge" V-8. 4. Dodge's tacked-on fins made for a peculiar profile in '59, when a Custom Royal Lancer convertible stickered at $3422.

4

1. Oh, the choices! A 1960 Dodge Dart Phoenix could have anything from a sturdy Slant Six (*right*) to a robust D-500 383-cid V-8 (*above left*). **2.** Models were renamed for 1960, with two ragtops making the cut: a plush Polara V-8 at $3416 (shown) and smaller Dart Phoenix. **3.** Once again in '61, stylists took a unique approach to Dodge fins. Stranger yet, the Polara ragtop dropped in price. **4.** Dodges shrunk in size and weight for 1962, but customers failed to respond. With Ram Induction, the V-8 in a Polara 500 made up to 330 horsepower. **5.** In its final season as a mid-size model, the 1962 Dart 440 convertible offered buyers a choice of four V-8s.

1

3

4

5

1. Dodges exhibited a cleaner shape for 1963, when five convertibles went on sale; the Polara ranked right in the middle. **2.** Reduced to compact dimensions for 1963, a Dodge Dart convertible came in either mid-range 270 or bucket-seat GT trim. **3.** A 1964 Polara convertible served as the Hurst lead car at the 1964 NHRA Winternational drag races. Even the model's hat featured a replica Hurst gear shift. **4.** In 1964, the Polara 500 line included a pair of hardtops and a convertible, with V-8 power only. **5.** Dodge's biggest '64 car was the Custom 880, introduced during 1962 and offered in a slew of body styles, including a convertible.

1

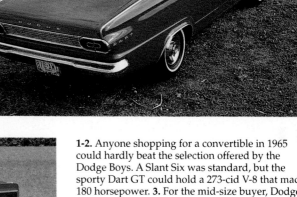

2

3

1-2. Anyone shopping for a convertible in 1965 could hardly beat the selection offered by the Dodge Boys. A Slant Six was standard, but the sporty Dart GT could hold a 273-cid V-8 that made 180 horsepower. **3.** For the mid-size buyer, Dodge had a trio of ragtops for '65, topped by the $2894 Coronet 500. A 180-horsepower V-8 was standard, but options reached all the way to 330 bhp. **4.** Redesigned for 1965, the $3335 Custom 880 again ranked as Dodge's biggie but rode the same wheelbase as a Polara or Monaco. Most big-engined convertibles exhaled via dual pipes.

4

1

2

1. In 1968, an energetic Dodge Coronet R/T (Road/Track) convertible listed for $3613, with 375 horses rarin' to kick up the dirt. Dodge established a sound reputation for middle-priced muscle. Sophisticated ragtop fans had several less-brazen choices at dealerships. 2. Only a GT convertible went on sale in the 1967 Dart series, with a Slant Six or small-block V-8. 3. Coronet R/T ragtops hit the market for the last time in 1970. This multi-scooped example has the rare, optional Hemi V-8.

3

1

2

1. Dodge's first convertibles of the Eighties had no quarter windows, but those were added to the 1984 Dodge 600. Paying an extra $2300 brought buyers a new turbo engine. 2. Turning from luxury to performance for its strong-selling convertible, Dodge issued the 600 ES Turbo in 1985, with a sport/handling suspension and 60-series tires. 3. For its final outing in 1986, the Dodge 600 earned a crossbar-style grille. Shoppers snapped up 11,678 base models and 4759 of the hotter ES Turbos. 4. Starting at $12,995 in 1991, the subcompact Dodge Shadow was America's lowest-priced convertible for a short while.

3

4

EDSEL

Judged by numbers alone, Edsel convertibles would warrant barely a footnote in automotive history. Only 4225 open Edsels left the factory over the make's three-season lifespan—too many to rank as rare, but not enough to qualify as a success. What makes them intriguing, of course, is the fact that the Edsel badge, introduced with such high hopes and heavy investment, so quickly became a virtual synonym for failure.

Was the ill-fated Edsel truly a "bad" car? Not really. Sure, critics found a fault or two—including an overabundance of power in top models. But taken as a whole, Edsel can be seen as typical of its time—a period of excess, when few automobiles escaped reviewers' well-honed hatchets.

Ford developed the medium-priced Edsel because it perceived a gap in the Ford-Mercury-Lincoln triumvirate. And in those glory days of healthy car sales, gaps were meant to be filled. Ford's mistake lay in not anticipating that the mid-price market might falter, which is exactly what happened as Americans endured a severe recession in 1958, the Edsel's opening season.

Executives considered some 6000 names for the new make—including "Utopian Turtletop," an inane suggestion from poet Marianne Moore. Eventually, Ford settled on Edsel, honoring the only son of company founder Henry Ford and father of then-president Henry Ford II. Edsel Ford had died in 1943.

Four series made up the 1958 Edsel line. The lowest-priced Ranger and step-up Pacer, on a 118-inch wheelbase, were related to concurrent Ford models. Corsairs and Citations, riding a 124-inch span and carrying a 345-horsepower, 410-cid V-8 engine that whipped out an overly eager 475 pound-feet of torque, had a closer kinship to Mercury models. No convertible was offered in the Ranger or Corsair series, but a Pacer droptop sold for $3028, and a top-of-the-line Citation commanded $3801. Only 930 open Citations came off the line but twice as many Pacers.

Judged in 1958 terms, Edsels were less gaudy and ostentatious than many rivals. Horizontal taillights and a vertical-motif grille soon inspired caustic comments—some witty, others crude, from psychologists as well as regular motorists. Edsels were packed with gadgetry, including Teletouch pushbutton controls for the automatic transmission in the steering-wheel hub, and a "cyclops eye" rotating-drum speedometer.

Launched in a flurry of publicity, the Edsel sold reasonably well in its first months. Despite the recession, model-year production totaled 63,110 cars.

That was far below Ford's expectations, so the lineup was trimmed to two series for 1959, on a single 120-inch wheelbase. Styling was toned down, as well. Just one convertible made the cut this time—a $3072 Corsair, with 1343 produced. Corsairs now had a 332-cid V-8 that developed 225 horsepower, with a 303-bhp, 361-cid engine optional. Low-budget Rangers could even have six-cylinder power instead of any V-8, but no ragtops wore a Ranger badge.

The badging situation changed for the 1960 model year when a paltry 76 Ranger convertibles were issued—the only series that season, except for Villager station wagons. Actually, production ground to a halt in November 1959, just after the cut-priced, reduced-content 1960 models went on sale.

DRAMATIC EDSEL STYLING leads the way
—in distinction, in beauty, in value!

Last August, the photograph above could not have been taken. The Edsel car was still a secret then. But in one short year, Edsel's outstanding design has become as familiar as it is distinctive. In fact, you can recognize the classic Edsel lines much faster, much farther away, than you can any other car in America! This extra value in advanced styling accounts for the many more Edsels you've been seeing on the road lately.

And proud new Edsel owners are getting plenty of extra value *inside* their cars, too—the ease of Teletouch Drive, the power and economy of the all-new engines, the convenience of self-adjusting brakes, the comfort of contour seats. And the satisfaction of having made a great buy. For there's less than fifty dollars difference between the magnificent Edsel and V-8's of the major low-priced makes.*

Why not see your Edsel Dealer this week for sure?

E D S E L   D I V I S I O N   •   F O R D   M O T O R   C O M P A N Y

Less than fifty dollars between Edsel and V-8's of the major low-priced makes *Based on comparison of manufacturers' suggested retail delivered prices.*

1

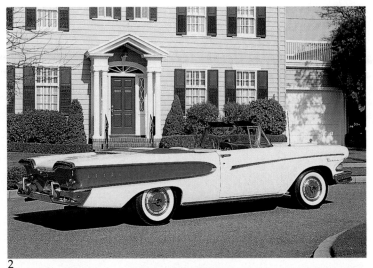

2

3

4

1-2. Despite staunch criticism, especially in later years, the ill-fated Edsel fit right into its era, with an easy-to-spot upright grille and "gullwing" deck. Adapting structural details from Ford, 1958 Pacers held a 303-horsepower, 361-cid V-8 engine. Just 1876 were convertibles. 3-4. First-year Citation ragtops sold half as well as Pacers, but the 410-cid V-8 yielded a burly 475 pound-feet of torque. Note the factory-installed spotlights. 5. Though derided as gimmicks, Teletouch Drive buttons in the steering-wheel hub seemed to make sense. Edsel options included a tach and compass.

5

1

2

3

4

1. After a disappointing 1958 selling season, only a single Edsel convertible went to dealerships in 1959. Just 1343 Corsair ragtops were produced, as price cuts failed to trigger the totals needed to keep the new make alive. That year's Mile-O-Matic transmission lost its pushbutton controls, and a more orthodox speedometer was installed. **2.** Styling was less distinctive, if more appealing, in 1959, featuring conventional taillights and a slightly subdued but still-vertical grille. A 361-cid V-8 cost $58 extra and demanded premium fuel but produced 303 horses—same as the '58 Pacer. **3-4.** Only a handful of Ranger convertibles rolled out the door for a brief 1960 season, out of 2846 cars in all. A hopeless catch phrase—"new-nifty-thrifty" Edsels—didn't help at all. Note the vertical taillights and matching back-up lights and the split horizontal grille. Two- and three-speed automatic transmissions were available. Either of two V-8 engines might be installed, but some Edsels had six-cylinder powerplants.

FORD

In 1929, as the Model A replaced the long-lived Model T, Ford issued a rumble-seat cabriolet. Sales beat those of all other American convertibles combined. Into the Thirties, Ford sold more convertibles than anyone—coupes as well as sedans.

A new flathead V-8 in 1932 further sealed Ford's position as sales victor. Convertible sedans hung on through 1939. By 1941, Ford's convertible was in the top Super DeLuxe series. Popular? Ford managed to move 30,240 ragtops that season. After World War II, Ford had a surprise ready: not only a plain steel-bodied convertible but also a wood-trimmed Sportsman. Doors, rear fenders, and deck were framed with white ash and mahogany. From 1946 to '48, Ford built 3485 of these, which cost some $500 more than a plain ragtop.

Sleeker, modern bodies arrived in 1949, and Ford's Custom V-8 convertible turned into the most popular open car of the season. More than 51,000 went to customers, helping Ford wrest the total-sales lead from Chevrolet. Restyled again for 1952, Fords were lower and smoother, and the Sunliner convertible bowed in the top Crestline series (again V-8 only). Into the mid-Fifties, Ford readied a radical design or two.

First came Thunderbird, in 1955: a "personal" two-seater with roll-down windows, a Mercury-based V-8, and bolt-on hardtop. More of a "boulevard" car than Chevrolet's Corvette, which evolved into a full-bore sports car, the T-Bird nevertheless captured the hearts of many.

Then, in 1957, Ford offered the Skyliner, the sole mass-market example of a steel-topped, retractable hardtop. Unlike cars from rival automakers, who used the "hardtop convertible" designation loosely, Ford's Skyliner truly deserved that title. The complicated system allowed the roof to disappear into the Skyliner's tall deck after its hinged front flap folded out of the way.

Thunderbirds expanded and added a back seat for 1958. Hardtop coupes outsold the convertibles by a wide margin. Full-size Fords earned restyling for 1959, and again in 1960 and '61. In 1962, a Galaxie 500 convertible cost $2924, while $3518 bought a sportier, bucket-seated 500/XL. On the T-Bird front, Ford issued 1882 Sports Roadsters in 1962–63, their back seats covered by a fiberglass tonneau with faired-in headrests.

The compact Falcon went topless in 1963, highlighted by a Sprint edition with bucket seats and a small-block V-8. By the middle of the Sixties, Ford ranked Number One in convertible production, due mainly to the wildly popular new Mustang. A whopping 101,945 Mustang ragtops went on sale during the model's extra-long initial season.

In 1966, Ford had eight convertibles on the market, but the total dropped to six in 1970— and none after '73. Fairlane convertibles joined in 1966, evolving into the Torino, whose convertible expired after 1971. Full-size ragtops lasted into '72, leaving Mustang as the only open Ford in 1973.

A decade later, the Mustang convertible was back, with a four-cylinder engine (turbo available), V-6, or 302-cid V-8. Through 1993, regular and GT ragtops went on sale. Curvaceously redesigned for 1994, Mustangs continue to tempt lovers of sporty rear-drive machinery; a Lincoln-based 4.6-liter V-8 was added for 1996.

FORD'S OUT FRONT!
with all 'round performance!

Best performing engines!

Only Ford gives you a choice of two great engines—the famous V-8 or the brilliant, new Ford Six! Both are power-packed performers. Both have balanced carburetion and new, 4-ring aluminum pistons for real thrift. Both engines make fewer revolutions per mile for longer life.

Best-built body!

Only Ford in its field has the "Lifeguard" Body—all-steel, all-welded for extra strength . . . rustproofed and finished in Ford baked enamel to keep its "showroom complexion." Underneath, there's the rugged Ford X-frame, plus "King-sized" Ford brakes for smooth, sure straight-line stops.

Best looking, inside & out!

Look at those smart Ford lines . . . then step inside and see the rest! Handsomest instrument panel in the low-priced field, with sparkling plastics, colorful controls. Sleek, streamlined fittings. Big, luxurious seats, upholstered in rich broadcloth or long-wearing mohair. Plenty of room—and comfort, too, thanks to Ford "Rest-ride" springs. Yes, Ford's out front in style!

Listen to the Ford Show starring Dinah Shore on Columbia Network stations Wed. evenings.

There's a *Ford* in your future

FORD

1. Like all Model A Fords, the new 1929 cabriolet held a 40-horsepower four-cylinder engine. Sales were brisk. 2. Priced at $625, the 1930 cabriolet was one of 18 body styles. 3. A 1931 Model A convertible sedan, with fixed roof rails, cost $640. More than 5000 customers drove one home. Ford also sold 13,706 cabriolets. 4. A new 221-cid V-8 helped enhance the appeal of the rumble-seat cabriolet, which went to 7062 buyers in 1932. 5. "Suicide" doors gave the '34 V-8 cabriolet a slightly sinister look. 6. This Ford convertible sedan paced the Indianapolis 500 race in 1935. Captain Eddie Rickenbacker (*in straw hat*) owned the track.

2

1

3

4

5

6

1. In addition to the 1935 DeLuxe cabriolet (shown), Ford continued to offer a roadster and phaeton. Shoppers snapped up 17,000 cabriolets. 2. Just 4234 Ford fans paid $580 to put a luscious 1935 convertible sedan in the garage. 3. Few cars sent young hearts thumping faster than a 1936 DeLuxe cabriolet, its rumble seat ready for sunny summer drives, and available luggage rack handy for long treks. This $625 coupe accounted for 14,068 sales, but the new club cabriolet added a regular back seat—a sign of things to come. The trunkback convertible sedan cost $780.
4. Roadsters faced their final season in 1937, but phaetons hung on longer. This DeLuxe convertible sedan sold for $859. Cabriolets again came with either a rumble seat or back bench, and the V-8 made 85 horsepower. 5. Rumble seats were fading from favor, but the $770 DeLuxe convertible coupe had one in 1938. Note the door-hinge mirrors. A convertible sedan then cost $900.

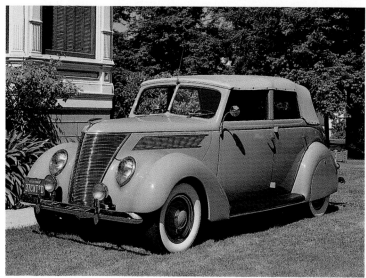

1

2

3

4

1. For the last time, in 1939, Ford offered a convertible sedan—with plenty of space for young passengers. More than 3500 went on sale, but open coupes sold three times as fast. 2. Fender skirts made a sharp Ford even slicker. A 1939 DeLuxe convertible coupe cost $788, versus $921 for the open sedan. 3. Only a DeLuxe convertible coupe was available in 1940, at $849, but 23,704 went to dealers. A column gearshift replaced the floor lever. 4. A V-8 Super DeLuxe convertible cost only $15 more than the new six in 1941. 5. Real wood decorated the '46 Sportsman, which typically went out the door loaded with extras. 6. By 1948, the Sportsman cost $2282, and only a handful of these final examples went on sale.

5

6

1. New slab-sided styling induced 51,133 admirers to select a 1949 convertible, sold only with V-8 power. Skirts cost extra. **2.** Company chief Henry Ford II (*at wheel*) posed with his brothers, Benson and William Clay, in the one millionth 1949 Ford—which happened to be a convertible. **3.** Ford had a Victoria hardtop in 1951, but the Custom V-8 convertible attracted nearly 21,000 customers. **4.** "Uncle" Tom McCahill, the witty auto tester for *Mechanix Illustrated*, took the wheel of a 1953 model. **5.** As the bodyside lettering suggests, a 1953 Sunliner paced that year's Indy 500 race. Note the simulated continental spare tire. **6.** A new overhead-valve V-8 went into the 1954 Sunliner.

1

2

3

4

5

6

FORD

1. Restyling for 1955 boosted the appeal of Ford's Sunliner, now in the Fairlane series; nearly 50,000 went on sale. Ragtops started at $2224, but a 272-cid V-8 with 162 or 182 horsepower was an extra-cost option. 2. Touched-up for 1956, a Sunliner might have six cylinders—or a "Thunderbird Special" 312-cid V-8, as performance options became the rule. Fords offered new safety features, but customers failed to respond. 3. Introduced a year earlier, the "personal" Thunderbird added a continental spare tire for 1956. A 292-cid V-8 was standard, with 312-cid engines available. T-Birds started at $3151 and sold 15,631 copies. 4. Ford went radical in 1957 with the Skyliner retractable hardtop. Priced at $2942 with standard 272-cid V-8, it cost $437 more than a regular ragtop, but 20,766 customers liked the idea of mixing fun-in-the-sun with a solid roof. The mechanism was complex, but no other automaker offered anything similar. 5. The 312-cid V-8 installed in 1957 Thunderbirds packed 245 to 300 horsepower—the latter figure achieved by supercharging. Only a handful of blown 'birds were sold.

1

2

3

4

5

1

2

3

4

6

7

5

8

1. Convertible production slipped in 1958, when the Fairlane Sunliner started at $2650. **2.** A 1957 Chevrolet may be more coveted today, but Ford's Fairlane 500 Sunliner drew more buyers at the time. Continental spares and skirts were popular. **3.** More than 77,000 Fairlane 500 Sunliners went on sale in '57. **4.** Thunderbirds turned into four-seaters for 1958, and the new hardtops proved more popular than ragtops. **5.** Thunderbirds could get a 430-cid V-8 in 1959. **6.** For 1959, Sunliners adopted the Galaxie badge. This one has the top V-8, packing 300 horses. **7.** Fords got horizontal fins for 1960. **8.** Thunderbird ragtops attracted 10,516 fans in 1961.

101

1

2

1. Brightwork grew gaudier for 1961. This Galaxie Sunliner has a factory continental spare and a 220-horsepower, 352-cid V-8. 2. In addition to a regular 1962 convertible, the Galaxie 500 line included a sporty 500/XL, with a 405-horsepower, 406-cid V-8 as top choice. 3. The Thunderbird Sports Roadster cost $5439 in 1962. Kelsey-Hayes wire wheels were standard. 4. Only 455 T-Bird Sports Roadsters were issued in 1963. Buyers liked the look enough to forgo the convenience of a back seat. 5. Ford's "Super Torque" 1963 lineup included the Galaxie 500/XL, which helped establish a "think young" trend. 6. The compact Falcon added a Futura Sprint ragtop in 1963, with a 164-bhp, 260-cid V-8.

3

4

5

6

1

2

3

4

5

1. Restyled for 1964, Thunderbirds featured a "projectile" front end. A complex mechanism sent the soft top into the rear-hinged trunk. 2. Falcon Sprint convertibles in 1964 had the 260-cid V-8. Regular ragtops held six-cylinder engines, and cost $190 less. 3. Ford launched the Mustang in April 1964, as a 1964 ½ model. Their long-hood/short-deck shape set the trend for what became known as "ponycars." 4. The 1965 Mustang convertible started at $2589, but most had a 289-cid V-8 and other extras. Popular at first, ragtops soon were eclipsed by hardtops and fastbacks. 5. Thunderbirds didn't change much for 1965. All ran with a 300-bhp, 390-cid V-8.

1

2

3

4

5

1. Fake fender vents departed from 1966 Thunderbirds, yielding a cleaner look. Only 5049 convertibles were built, versus 64,127 hardtops. The standard 390-cid V-8 made 315 horsepower. **2.** Full-size Fords changed more for 1965 than they had since '49. Production of the Galaxie 500/XL convertible dropped to 9849 cars, down from more than 15,000 the previous year. **3.** For 1966, mid-size Fairlanes finally came in convertible form, led by the 500/XL GT, packing a 335-bhp, 390-cid V-8. **4.** Taillights stretched full-width on the 1966 Thunderbird. This one has the newly optional 428-cid engine. **5.** A 1966 Ford Galaxie 500/XL convertible cost $3480, while $2934 bought a regular Galaxie ragtop. Equipped with a 428-cid engine, the convertible adopted a "7 Litre" designation.

1

2

1. Little-changed for 1966, the Mustang convertible started at $2653, and 72,119 were produced—against more than half a million hardtops.
2. Mustangs got a deeper grille for '67, as convertible output began to skid.
3. Popularity of the Galaxie 500/XL sagged in 1967, as 5161 ragtops went to dealers. This one has the 345-bhp, 428-cid V-8. 4. Mustangs could have a wide range of V-8s in 1968, from 289- to 427- or 428-cid. Note the luggage rack—one of many extra-cost accessories. 5. Performance fans could buy Mustangs modified by Carroll Shelby. (See Shelby chapter for details.)

3

4

5

1

2

3

4

5

1. A new Torino series joined the mid-size Fairlane for 1968, and a convertible paced the Indy 500. 2. Interest in sporty full-size models had been dwindling, so Ford issued a Galaxie 500/XL for the last time in 1970. 3. Only one Torino ragtop made the 1970 lineup: a GT with a 220-bhp, 302-cid V-8. Eye-popping paint was designed to lure the youth market. 4. Enlarged for the second time, the 1971 Mustang ragtop weighed 600 pounds more than the original. 5. Patriotic striping marked the 1972 Mustang Sprint. 6. Last of the big open Mustangs, the '73 could have a 351-cid Cobra Jet V-8 and Ram Air hood.

6

1. By 1987, the revived Mustang convertible had been around for five seasons. An LX could have either a four-cylinder engine or 302-cid (5.0-liter) V-8, while the GT came only with the 225-horsepower V-8. **2.** In 1986, the Mustang GT started at $14,523, while $12,821 bought an LX with V-6 power. After shrinking in 1974, Mustangs had been redesigned—and enlarged—for 1979. **3.** By 1993, the Mustang design was getting old. Convertibles came in LX trim, with four cylinders or a 205-horsepower V-8 (named the 5.0L). A GT listed for $20,848, including the V-8 plus a front air dam and rear spoiler. **4.** In 1995, a Mustang ragtop stickered at $20,795 while a GT went for $22,595. **5.** Mustangs showed off a rounded redesign for 1994 but retained the familiar rear-drive layout. Either a 3.8-liter V-6 or 5.0-liter V-8 was available. Note the scoop ahead of the rear wheel on this GT—one of several assertive touches for the Nineties.

1

2

3

4

5

HUDSON-
ESSEX-TERRAPLANE

A convertible first wore a Hudson emblem in 1928, though the sedan-based bodywork came from an outside supplier. A year later Essex, Hudson's lower-priced mate, joined the convertible crowd. Next came an Essex Challenger Six Sun Sedan. In 1932 an open coupe joined the Essex Pacemaker line. Hudson itself offered a rumble-seated convertible that year, in its Greater Eight series, abandoning roadster and phaeton body styles.

On July 21, 1932, two months after becoming the first woman to fly solo across the Atlantic, Amelia Earhart christened the first Essex Terraplane and drove home the second car off the line. Quick and stylish, Terraplanes delivered the highest power-to-weight ratio of any production automobile. In 1933, convertibles were offered in each Essex Terraplane series. The Essex prefix was dropped in 1934, and that nameplate disappeared altogether. Through the mid-Thirties, Terraplanes gave Hudson a sporty, youthful, moderately priced product to rival the swift Ford V-8s.

Hudson had taken a little longer than some makes to adopt streamlined styling, but when it did, the results were stunning. Output rose nearly 50 percent in 1934, after plummeting sharply through the early Thirties. Hudsons and Terraplanes had the option of a Bendix-designed "Electric Hand" in 1935, which allowed fingertip gearshift control.

By 1938, the Terraplane—now a Hudson series rather than a separate make—was in its final season, still offered in convertible coupe and Brougham form. Counterparts continued in the larger Hudson lines—Six and Eight.

Hudson called its ragtops "convertible sedans" in the late prewar period, but the cars had only two doors instead of the typical sedan's four. Unlike most, Hudson's 1941–42 convertibles were engineered to be as solid as actual sedans, using a heavily reinforced frame. By then, a power mechanism operated the soft top, and detachable rear quarter windows gave way to glass that lowered along with the roof.

Convertibles reappeared following the production break mandated by World War II. Then, in 1948, came "Step-down" styling—Hudson's giant step into a futuristic stance. Low and lithe, the unibodied Step-downs demonstrated great strength, and Hudsons gained a reputation as peerless highway drivers. Again branded "broughams," the convertibles differed from all other ragtops. Thick steel windshield headers betrayed the fact that they'd been adapted from closed bodies, but this allowed Hudson to tout the design's rollover protection.

Hudson hit the stock-car circuits full-bore in 1951, when the extra-hot Hornet arrived, carrying the biggest six-cylinder engine on the market. Coupes did race duty, but convertibles, too, had the option of 308 cubic inches and 145 horsepower.

Hornet and Super Wasp ragtops continued into 1954, when the Step-down design enjoyed a final touch-up. After the merger with Nash, the final Hudsons (1955–57) were little more than rebadged Nashes; these included Hollywood hardtops but no convertibles. A handful of Hudson Metropolitans (imported from England) served as the last open cars to carry Hudson badging.

Here's where your heart skips a beat!

The modern design for '49

A magnificent New Hudson Convertible ready for your inspection

HERE, beyond all doubt, is the most elegant convertible American motor-car artistry has ever conceived for assembly line production!

The long, sweeping lines of this magnificent automobile, its gorgeous interior appointments, chaste chrome fittings, and rich leather or special combination of leather and fabric upholstery, mark it as a car you can own and drive with deep and enduring pride.

Over and above its beauty and luxury, you will find many notable and fundamental advances in convertible construction in this remarkable car.

This convertible has unexcelled riding qualities and a new measure of safety, both largely resulting from the fact that it has the lowest center of gravity in any American stock car—yet road clearance is ample!

Even with this lower center of gravity and the car's new, low silhouette, there is *generous head room* with the top up, because Hudson floors are recessed down within a base frame. Hudson is the only car you step *down* into!

Outward vision with the top up is greatly increased, not only through a wide, curved windshield and generous side windows, but also through a new type "FOLD-AWAY"‡ rear window that is 100 per cent larger than usual, and is invisibly hinged across its plate-glass area so that it folds down into the body with the top.*

There is a beautifully symmetrical new windshield header that not only contributes to the remarkable overall rigidity of this convertible, but also nests a Pullman-type interior map light, twin sun visors, and a radio antenna control knob, all instantly available for use, yet protected and out of the way where they do not impair vision.

Everything possible is provided for your convenience and ease. A touch of your finger on a button automatically raises or lowers the top and windows*, and the well which receives the top as it is lowered is enclosed with leather-fabric panelling, and carpeted for parcel storage when the top is up.

Among the many options available in this new convertible, is Hudson's Drive-Master automatic transmission** which provides the easiest of all ways to drive. At the turn of a button on the instrument panel, you have your choice of three driving methods . . . conventional drive, manual shifting without use of the clutch, or fully automatic gear shifting in forward speeds.

This outstanding motor car was conceived and built to thrill you right down to your toes! Hudson dealers will gladly show it to you at your earliest convenience. Hudson Motor Car Company, Detroit 14.

*Standard on the Commodore, an optional extra on the Super
**An optional extra available on all New Hudson models

New Safety through a large, newly developed, plate-glass window, which gives 100 per cent more rear vision and is invisibly hinged so that it folds snugly down into the body with the top when not in use! No other convertible offers the advantages of this "FOLD-AWAY"‡ window, which is built into a cloth section that is "zippered" into the top*. Top materials are black, red or gray to harmonize with your choice of several sparkling new body colors.

Unique Windshield header described in the text of this advertisement is illustrated above.

Both Commodore Eight and Super-Six upholstered in rich, antique red leather, with an optional choice at no extra cost of leather and cloth combination—the cloth being a new, specially treated, water-repellent, worsted Bedford Cord in two selections of three-tone colors. Super-Cushion, low-pressure tires standard; white sidewalls an optional extra.

‡Patents applied for

The only car you step down into

Hudson

Copyright 1948, Hudson Motor Car Co.

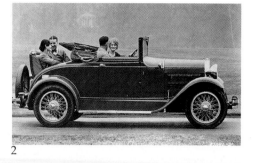

1

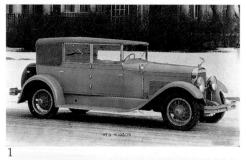

2

3

4

5

6

1. The Murphy Body company did the coachwork for this upright but handsome 1928 Hudson convertible Landau sedan. 2. A convertible coupe highlighted the Essex line in 1929. The gentleman in back looks eager to "spoon." 3. Essex added a Sun Sedan for 1930. Note the high spotlights on this one. 4. Famed aviatrix Amelia Earhart took delivery of this 1933 Essex Terraplane convertible coupe. 5. One of five 1933 Essex convertibles, this Model KT held a 94-horsepower, 244-cid straight eight engine. 6. Hudson products could be at home anywhere. Lady Astor posed with a right-hand-drive 1933 Essex Terraplane convertible, sporting a low windshield.

1

2

3

4

5

1. Not many 1934 cars looked as rakish as a Terraplane K Special Six convertible coupe—sharper yet with skirts and sidemounts. Independent front suspension became a no-cost option. 2. A 1935 Terraplane Deluxe convertible with an 88-horsepower six cost $725. Note the "suicide" doors. 3. In DeLuxe Eight form, a 93-bhp 1936 Hudson convertible coupe went for $875. Hudsons rode a 120-inch wheelbase, versus 115 for Terraplanes. 4. A 113-horsepower engine went into the 1936 Hudson Custom Eight convertible. "Duo-Automatic" brakes were hydraulic, with a mechanical backup. 5. Hudson Eight broughams for 1937 came in DeLuxe or Custom trim.

1

2

3

4

5

6

1. Terraplane got front-hinged doors for 1937, as wheelbases grew to 117 inches and body widths expanded. **2.** Each 1942 Hudson series had a convertible, including this $1402 Commodore Six. **3.** Hudson called its postwar ragtops "broughams." This 1946 Super Six cost $1879, and sold far better than the Commodore Eight. **4-5.** Step-down styling gave the 1949 Commodore Six Brougham a unique appearance, led by a thick windshield header. Convertibles also came in the Super Six and Commodore Eight series. **6.** To mark Hudson's 40th anniversary, president A.E. Barit took the wheel of a 1949 Commodore Brougham, ahead of a 1909 Hudson Model 20.

1. Hudson issued a total of 1651 convertibles for 1951, in each of five series—including the hot new Hornet, which packed 145 horsepower. 2. Hudson restyled its Step-down shape for 1954, offering a pair of Brougham convertibles: a Hornet (shown) and Super Wasp. 3-4. Wire wheel covers and a spotlight were among the extra-cost accessories available to decorate a 1954 Hornet Brougham. Note the abundant bright trim, including small fender skirts. 5. By 1954, the Hornet's 308-cid six-cylinder engine with Twin H-Power (dual carburetors) developed 160 horsepower—or 170 horses in 7-X racing tune. Many Hornets had Hydra-Matic, but overdrive also was popular.

1

2

3

4

5

KAISER-FRAZER

Prior to World War II, shipbuilder Henry J. Kaiser had been experimenting with plastic-bodied automobiles. Joseph W. Frazer was an auto-industry veteran, who bought the abandoned Graham-Paige company in 1944. In July 1945, these two dissimilar yet ambitious men joined forces and formed Kaiser-Frazer, ready to produce the first all-new car of the postwar era. Kaiser would be the manufacturing whiz, while Frazer's greatest gifts lay in sales.

Styling emanated largely from the pen of Howard A. "Dutch" Darrin. A handful of early Frazers were assembled at the Old Graham-Paige facility. Then, in June 1946, full production of 1947 Kaisers and Frazers commenced at Willow Run, Michigan, in a bomber plant that Henry Kaiser had purchased from Ford.

Each make consisted of just one body style: a slab-sided, flush-fendered four-door sedan—superficially ordinary, yet different from anything on the market, for nearly every rival automaker had only lightly facelifted clones of 1942 models.

Kaiser was the mid-priced model, starting at $1868 for the Special sedan, but quickly raised to $2104 as postwar inflation ran rampant. A Custom sedan ran $352 higher. Frazers began at $2295, jumping to $2712 for the luxurious Manhattan. A 226-cid flathead six-cylinder engine powered both models. In the postwar seller's market—with shoppers eager to snap up anything on wheels—Kaisers sold well, and Frazers fared not too badly. When Henry and Joe decided to try their hand at an open car, they had only the four-door body and no free funds to develop a two-door. So, the four-door served as a basis for one of the most unorthodox ragtops issued by an American manufacturer—a convertible sedan, at a time when other manufacturers had abandoned that idea years before.

Because the convertible's windshield header was adapted from the sedan's roof, it was thicker than most, though not as broad as that of the "Step-down" Hudson design introduced for 1948. A few test runs in the prototype demonstrated that the sedan's chassis lacked sufficient rigidity, so Kaiser-Frazer adopted a reionforced X-frame.

Even that wasn't enough to assure structural integrity, so body engineer John Widman recommended structural B-pillars. Neither the metal-framed glass panels nor the chrome side-window frames could be removed or retracted. Each piece remained in position, whether the convertible top was up or down.

Only 124 convertibles were produced in 1949–50. About 70 were Frazer Manhattans, and the rest Deluxe Kaisers. An open Kaiser cost $3195—no small sum in those days—while the Manhattan brought $100 more. Kaiser also issued more than 900 hardtop sedans, using the same theme.

Another 131 convertible sedans went on sale in 1951, all Frazer Manhattans. Actually, they were leftover 1950 models, with revised front and rear ends that weren't likely to win any beauty contests at the time.

Although second-generation Kaisers, introduced in 1951, looked luscious, no convertible was in the cards. A prototype was built, but the foundering company had no money for such frivolities. Kaiser focused instead on the new compact Henry J, which, like the firm itself, lasted only a few more years. No Frazers were issued after 1951 and the final Kaisers went on sale in 1955.

...in a 1949 FRAZER CONVERTIBLE

Tuck her in next to you...touch a button and watch the FRAZER top slide away automatically...be off with the wind to your own wooded wonderland! And if the rest of the crowd *must* come along, both the front and rear seats are wide, wide, *wide*—with *lots* of leg room. For you're driving the new 1949 FRAZER *Convertible*—the only full-size four-door *convertible* on the road! Big, handsome—a *dream* of a car! Yours in more colors than a pastel rainbow...yours in practically any fabric or leather-type interior you could imagine. You provide the girl...the nearest KAISER-FRAZER dealer will have the new 1949 FRAZER *Convertible* soon! Kaiser-Frazer Corporation, Willow Run, Michigan.

See it today—and drive it away! The new 1949 FRAZER with 100 new features, improvements and refinements—at your dealer's NOW!

"THE BEAUTY AND DISTINCTION OF CUSTOM CAR STYLING"

1

3

4

2

1. Even though the fabric top on a '49 Kaiser Virginian convertible sedan folded down, its window framework and glass-paned B-pillars remained in place. Only 54 were built, plus 946 four-door hardtops. No other automaker offered either body style. **2.** Ornate Kaiser dashboards, bedecked with brightwork, featured a giant speedometer and matching clock. Note the exposed trunk hinges. **3.** "Flax" script identified this Kaiser's body color. **4.** Frazer (*foreground*) and Kaiser convertible sedans each rode a 123.5-inch wheelbase, but Frazer Manhattans had standard skirts and a more intricate grille.

1

2

3

4

5

1. Engineers sheared the roof of a sedan to create the 1949 Frazer Manhattan convertible. **2.** Some Frazers had Hydra-Matic instead of a three-speed stick shift. **3.** Hydraulics operated the windows and top. **4.** Reworked for 1951, an open Frazer cost $3075. **5.** Sadly, only a prototype of the 1951 Kaiser convertible coupe was built.

LA SALLE

General Motors launched the LaSalle in March 1927, as a lower-priced companion to Cadillac. Why? Because GM president Alfred P. Sloan wanted to offer a GM car for every pocketbook, from low-budget Chevrolet to lush Cadillac, encompassing every step in between. The LaSalle was intended to fill a perceived gap between Buick and Cadillac. Powered by a smaller V-8 engine than Cadillac's, LaSalles also rode a shorter wheelbase. The luscious body was penned by legendary West Coast stylist Harley J. Earl, soon to become head of the corporation's newly-created Art & Colour Studio. Sloan lured Earl away from his West Coast position with one specific initial duty in mind: to sculpt the new "junior Cadillac."

Convertibles were part of the LaSalle lineup right from the start. In 1928, a LaSalle rumble-seat convertible sold for $2550. Its engine soon grew from the original 303 cubic inches to 328 cid, developing 86 horsepower. In 1930, the Fisher-bodied Series 340 convertible coupe went for $2590—exactly the same as a closed coupe. By then, LaSalles rode a 134-inch wheelbase, abandoning the original 125-inch "standard" span. The V-8 engine now measured 340 cid, rated at 90 horsepower. LaSalle prices ranged from $2490 to $3995, versus $3295 for the cheapest Cadillac.

As the Great Depression grew deeper, it was LaSalle that enabled Cadillac to stay afloat. In 1933, the rock-bottom year for the American economy, LaSalle outsold Cadillac by a modest margin.

LaSalle shed its Cadillac connection as part of a 1934 restyling. The new Series 350 had a look all its own, with basic bodyshells and 240-cid straight-eight engines borrowed from Oldsmobile. Prices and weights were slashed, and new Knee-Action independent front suspensions installed. A 2/4-passenger convertible coupe now cost $1695—same as the four-door sedan—down from $2395 in '33. By 1936, the Series 50 convertible dropped to just $1255.

Something new arrived in 1937: a five-passenger convertible sedan to accompany the open coupe. Cadillac engines went under LaSalle hoods once again: L-head 322-cid V-8s, developing 125 horsepower. Only 855 convertible coupes and 265 convertible sedans left the assembly line in 1938. The next year's totals came to 1056 and 185, respectively, out of more than 21,000 LaSalles.

Harley Earl again took pen in hand, coming up with one of the best-looking LaSalles ever. For a change, the 1940 models came in two series: 40-50 and 40-52 Special. Each series included both a convertible coupe and convertible sedan. Production of open "junior" editions totaled 724 (599 of them coupes), while the costlier Special included 425 two-door convertibles and 75 four-doors. Coupes gained vacuum-powered tops.

Although closed LaSalle coupes and sedans accounted for far more sales in 1940, the make was about to expire anyway. By then, a Series 62 Cadillac cost only a few hundred dollars more, whereas Buicks had edged well into the LaSalle's price range. So, instead of releasing a 1941 LaSalle, GM elected to offer a lower-priced Cadillac instead, the Series 61.

The LaSalle name was revived briefly in 1955 to designate a one-off two-seat roadster created for the '55 GM Motorama show. Now and then, the name is still bandied about for possible use on some new GM model.

Comprenez - vous ?...

SHARING FIRST PLACE WITH CADILLAC

When comparisons are suggested between lesser cars and the La Salle, it will pay to remember that the General Motors Corporation—manufacturer of the leading automobiles in every grade—is behind the creation of this especial value in automobiles. The La Salle shares with Cadillac the famous 90-degree, V-type, eight-cylinder engine—together with first place in the fine car field.

FOR A SMALL DOWN PAYMENT—with the appraisal value of your used car acceptable as cash—you may possess a La Salle on the liberal term-payment plan of the General Motors Acceptance Corporation—the famous G.M.A.C. plan.

CADILLAC MOTOR CAR COMPANY
DIVISION OF GENERAL MOTORS CORPORATION
DETROIT, MICHIGAN   OSHAWA, CANADA

LA SALLE
Priced from $2495 to $2685, f. o. b. Detroit

MANUFACTURED · COMPLETELY · BY · THE · CADILLAC · MOTOR · CAR · COMPANY · WITHIN · ITS · OWN · PLANTS

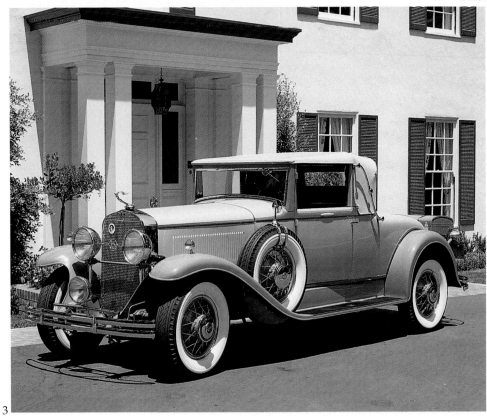

1

3

2

1. By including a convertible coupe at the time of its 1927 debut, LaSalle became one of the first makes to offer that body style. The 303-cid V-8 used in Series 303 yielded more than 75 horsepower. Sleek and low, LaSalles featured sweeping fenders and tall radiators, with spicy two-toning available. **2.** When Series 328 appeared during 1928, LaSalle's V-8 grew to 328 cubic inches. Hoods now held 28 narrow louvers instead of a dozen broad ones. **3-4.** In 1930, this splendid convertible coupe was one of seven Fisher body styles for Series 340. LaSalles were bigger, heavier, and more costly than many other convertibles. Note the auxiliary trunk and strapped-on mirror. **5.** Except for headlight shape, 1932 LaSalles were nearly identical to Cadillacs. The 353-cid V-8 in this Series 345B convertible made 115 horsepower.

4

5

1. By 1937, LaSalles were positioned as rivals to Packard's One Twenty series. A record 32,000 cars were built—far beyond previous totals. This Series 50 rumble-seat convertible coupe cost $1350 and weighed 3715 pounds. Similar in design to the previous year's Cadillac 60, LaSalles returned to V-8 power after a three-year flirtation with straight eights. Note the small, split rear window.
2. LaSalle dashboards contained a delicately graduated speedometer and matching clock.
3. Adroit restyling on a 124-inch wheelbase gave 1937 LaSalles a checkered, expansive hood trim and lower headlights. Through 1940, a convertible sedan also was available.

1

2

3

LINCOLN

Even before launching into the convertible arena, Lincolns were known for their fashionable appeal—an influence initiated by Edsel Ford, the ill-fated son of the company's founder. Lincoln's sport convertible, custom-bodied by Brunn, appeared at the New York Auto Show in 1927 with a $5000 price, identical to that of the Dietrich-bodied phaeton.

Dietrich, LeBaron, and other coachbuilders continued to ply their trade on Lincoln chassis as the Thirties decade began, turning out small quantities of convertible coupes and sedans. In 1932, the new KB Series carried a 448-cid V-12 engine. A year later, the prior V-8 was gone, replaced by a smaller Twelve. By 1934, prices of convertible coupes ranged from $3400 to $5600 and beyond. Brunn was responsible for most of the cabriolet and Victoria bodiess that were issued in the mid-Thirties, while LeBaron created convertible roadsters and sedans.

K-Series Lincolns with big V-12 engines remained available as late as 1940, but in dwindling numbers. Meanwhile, in 1936, Lincoln took a completely different turn, issuing smaller—and far cheaper—Zephyr sedans, with reduced-displacement V-12 engines. Convertibles joined the streamlined Zephyr lineup for 1938.

Edsel Ford came up with the idea of a Zephyr based Continental, leaving the design details to Bob Gregorie. Result: one of the most enduring classics of all time. Sleek yet formal in profile, Continentals featured a long hood and extra-short deck, with an outside spare tire at the rear. Starting in 1940, both a convertible (cabriolet) and a steel-roofed coupe went on sale.

Lincolns got a facelift for '42, and a more reliable 305-cid V-12 engine. After the war, though, the prior 292-cid V-12 returned to replace the 305. Production of the Continental cabriolet peaked in 1947, with 738 built—plus 831 coupes.

A far different Lincoln emerged for 1949. Dubbed "bathtub" in shape, they came in two sizes and carried plenty of weight—more than 4400 pounds for the Cosmopolitan convertible and only 200 less for its shorter-wheelbase mate. Only the Cosmo ragtop continued into 1950-51.

Lovely reshaping for 1952 gave Lincoln another personality—plus performance that permitted the cars to take the *Carrera Panamericana* (Mexican Road Race) by storm. Capri convertibles from 1952-54 were among the most graceful on the market. Not everyone said the same about the longer, wider Capri and Premiere that debuted in 1956, though the design won awards and sales almost doubled. The stylistically overwrought Continental Mark III was Lincoln's sole convertible in 1958, followed by a Mark IV and Mark V in 1959-60.

If the late Fifties Lincolns served as archetypes of wretched excess, the convertible sedan introduced in 1961 was archetypal elegance. Not since the Frazer a decade earlier had anyone turned out a four-door convertible, and Lincoln's was a masterpiece: smaller and lighter than the 1958-60 models, and crisply styled with knife-edge fenders. Its top moved smoothly beneath a hinged rear deck, using a system of 11 relays and scads of mechanical linkages. Continental convertible sedans hung on through 1967, though they looked a bit limp in later years. Since then, no Lincoln convertibles have been offered.

Nothing could be finer

THE LINCOLN CONTINENTAL CABRIOLET

When available, white sidewall tires at extra cost.

Lincoln

DIVISION OF FORD MOTOR COMPANY

1

2

1. It took a pretty penny to drive home a Dietrich-bodied convertible sedan in 1929—$6900, to be exact, at a time when Model A Fords started at $450. Landau bars, sidemounted spare tires, and a folding trunk rack were typical luxury-car extras in the late Twenties. Note the leaping hood ornament. 2. A 1934 Series KB convertible Victoria, bodied by Brunn, rode a 145-inch wheelbase. Series KA models used a 136-inch span. Lincoln's 414-cid V-12 developed 150 horsepower. Coachbuilt cars of this caliber easily topped 5000 pounds. 3. Custom-bodied Lincoln Series K convertible sedans in 1935 carried five passengers, and could be ordered on either wheelbase. 4. Introduced two years earlier, the mid-priced Zephyr for 1938 added a $1700 convertible coupe, along with a $1790 convertible sedan.

3

4

1. LeBaron constructed the coachwork for this 1939 Lincoln Series K convertible sedan, which was used as a salon car. Headlights were built into fenders. Long-wheelbase models could be ordered with a chauffeur's partition. **2-3.** Streamlined shaping of the Lincoln Zephyr looked particularly pleasing on open bodies. A 1939 Zephyr convertible coupe seated four and sold for $1747. Only 640 were built, along with 302 convertible sedans. Note the graceful hinge-mounted mirrors. Vestigial running boards now were covered by skirts, making the car look smoother yet.
4. Breathtaking was the word for the Lincoln Continental when it first appeared as a 1940 model. A car of this nature had been specially built for Edsel Ford in 1938–39, on the Zephyr platform. So many onlookers asked about it, that the company decided to produce a limited quantity of Continentals. Cabriolets initially sold for $2916.

1

2

3

4

1

2

3

1. Only 400 fortunate folks could afford to pay $3865 for the privilege of driving home a 1941 Lincoln Continental cabriolet. More than twice that many club coupes went on sale. Lincoln's 292-cid V-12 engine developed 120 horsepower. **2.** Lushly shaped Continentals grabbed all the publicity in 1941, but the regular Zephyr convertible was no slouch in the design department and carried the same mechanical components—for a thousand dollars less. Only 725 went to customers. **3.** For one year only, Lincoln's V-12 engine grew to 305 cubic inches and 130 horsepower. The 1942 Zephyr convertible coupe sold for $2150, but only 191 were produced. **4.** Just 136 Lincoln Continental cabriolets rolled into dealerships in the 1942 model year, which was cut short by America's entry into World War II. Maroon was a popular hue.

4

1

2

1. After the war, the Zephyr name no longer was used for Lincolns, but V-12 engines remained. In 1948, just 452 Lincoln convertible coupes went on sale, at $3142 apiece. Lincoln's 292-cid V-12 engine yielded 125 horsepower. 2. Lincoln Continentals got a brighter, busier grille for the postwar period. Which is classier? You decide. The 1948 Continental cabriolet sold for $4746, while the club coupe cost $4662. Pushbutton-operated doors first appeared on 1941 models. 3. Whether painted in bright or subdued tones, a '48 Continental cabriolet oozed elegance. No other American automaker used a V-12 engine, and even Lincoln soon abandoned the configuration.

3

LINCOLN

1. A new 336.7-cid flathead V-8 powered the "bathtub" 1949 Lincolns, producing 152 horsepower. Convertibles came in two sizes: a 121-inch wheelbase version (shown) and the larger Cosmopolitan series, on a 125-inch span. Selling prices were $3116 and $3948, respectively. This "baby" Lincoln contains a power seat, windows, antenna, and top, plus an overdrive transmission.
2-3. Last of the bathtub-style Lincolns was the 1951 Cosmopolitan—quite a sight in chartreuse, its V-8 yielding two more horsepower than before. Only 857 ragtops were assembled this year, priced at $3891 each. By now, Lincolns typically came with Hydra-Matic transmission. Note the tiny backup lights on the trunk lid.

2

1

3

1

2

3

4

1. A new 160-horsepower overhead-valve V-8 and ball-joint front suspension turned the 1952 Lincolns into greater-yet road machines. Fewer than 1200 Capri convertibles were produced, with a $3665 price tag. New features included an aircraft-style dash. 2. By 1953–54, Lincoln's 317.5-cid V-8 needed 205 horsepower to keep up with the luxury-car pack. The Capri convertible listed for $4031, and 1951 were built. 3. Larger in size but not lacking in grace, the '56 Lincoln came in Capri and top-of-the-line Premiere trim, but only the latter included a convertible. Engines grew to 368 cubic inches and 285 horsepower. 4. Canted fins stretched tall on the 1957 Premiere, following the industry trend. Lincoln eschewed gaudy two- and three-tone paint, but bright single colors added to the cars' allure. Ragtop prices hit a lofty $5381, but 3676 customers said "yes."

1

2

3

4

5

1. Continually rivaling Cadillac, Lincoln turned out its biggest cars ever for 1958, including the $6283 Continental Mark III convertible. 2. After a series of sumptuous, oversculpted "land yachts" in 1958–60, Lincoln launched the comely 1961 Continental convertible sedan. Top-flight workmanship matched the lovely lines. Just 2857 were built, at $6713—versus 22,303 hardtop sedans. 3. Continentals were costly, but the '62 convertible was touted as a "remarkable investment." 4. Lincoln's 430-cid V-8 made 300 horsepower in '62. 5. Adding a four-barrel carburetor boosted output of the 1963 engine to 320 bhp—and the price to $6916.

1

2

3

4

1. Continentals gained a facelift for 1964, but the unique body style—back doors that open toward the rear—continued to lure luxury convertible buyers. Wheelbases grew by three inches, widening the rear entry space. Lincoln issued 3328 convertible sedans but nearly ten times that many hardtop sedans. Flat side glass replaced the original's curved panes, and the soft top had a lower profile. 2. Except for a revised grille and standard front disc brakes, the 1965 Continental convertible sedan showed only modest change. Lincoln's experience with the open four-door body style prompted no other automakers to take a comparable plunge, making the 1961–67 Continentals as unique as the earlier Ford retractables. 3-4. Continentals grew longer and got curvier bodysides for 1966. The V-8 was enlarged, as well, to 462 cubic inches.

MERCURY

Edsel Ford gets credit for the Mercury's existence. Named for the swift "messenger of the gods," the first Merc—issued in 1939—served as Ford's direct rival to Buick, Oldsmobile, and Pontiac, as well as Dodge and DeSoto. Though slightly larger, costlier, and more powerful than a Ford, the Merc was similar in shape, although it sported features of its own. In its second season, a convertible sedan temporarily joined the open coupe.

After the war, Mercury followed Ford's lead in offering a wood-bodied Sportsman. Although Ford's open woody lasted three years, Mercury produced that body style only in 1946.

Restyling in 1949 gave Mercury what some called a "bathtub" profile, similar to the new Lincoln. Many thought the new shape looked a bit better in coupe form than as a convertible. The coupe, after all, is what actor-icon James Dean drove in *Rebel Without a Cause*. Even so, a record 16,765 ragtops rolled off the line.

If Mercury had served as a "small Lincoln" in 1949–51, it became a "big Ford" for '52. Convertibles came only in the most expensive series: Monterey in 1952–54, then Montclair. A lower-priced Custom version became available for 1956. Soft-top sales peaked in 1955–57.

A third convertible joined during 1957: the glitzy Turnpike Cruiser. Gadget-laden and garishly overstyled, it was the most noticeable Mercury of them all. Only 1265 Convertible Cruisers were built before the model faded into history. That left only an open pair for 1958–60: the base Monterey and upscale Park Lane. By '61, the Park Lane was gone, leaving only one ragtop. A Monterey Custom S-55 convertible debuted during 1962.

Mercury had launched the compact Comet in 1960, but no convertible version appeared until 1963. Comets then came in two levels, Custom and S-22, helping convertible production to top the 18,000 mark. Big Mercs earned a major reskin that season.

By 1964, the Park Lane designation was back, including a convertible. Comet's soft-top now was called Caliente, and the Monterey Custom rounded out the ragtop trio.

A Lincoln-like restyling of full-size models came in 1965, prompting Mercury to promise "fine cars in the Continental tradition." A year later, the S-55 became a separate series. Only 669 ragtops went on sale, and the next year's output dipped to 145 cars.

For 1966, Comets grew to mid-size dimensions, sold in both Caliente and Cyclone guise, the latter available in GT trim. Packing a 335-horse 390-cid V-8, the GT challenged such heavy-action rivals as the Pontiac GTO and Oldsmobile 4-4-2. A 427-cid V-8 joined the Cyclone option list in '67. A year later, the only open Merc below full-size was the Montego MX.

An all-new Marquis debuted for 1969 as the top-of-the-line Mercury. Only 2319 of the posh Mercs got a soft top. Mid-size convertibles evaporated after 1969; big convertibles hung on one more year. Cougars, meanwhile, doffed their tops starting in 1969, in base and XR-7 trim, surviving into 1973.

After many years without a convertible, Mercury offered a new Capri in the summer of 1990. Built in Australia, the mini-ragtop carried a 1.6-liter dual-cam engine. Before the 1995 model year arrived, the Capri disappeared like its larger ragtop predecessors.

DOWN THE ROAD TO *Spring!*

White sidewall tires extra

MERCURY CLUB CONVERTIBLE

A FLASH OF COLOR headed for high adventure. A silent car to carry two through soft, moon-shadowed night. Greeting to Spring—in a long, low car with the top down! A clean-lined car, as eager and fleet as youth itself—for people young in spirit. . . . It's a long way from the old-time open cars to this smoothly streamlined Mercury Club

Convertible. Snug top operates automatically —folds down out of sight or closes tightly against the weather. Front seat is regular sedan-width, generously planned for three big people. The rear seat brings guests in under cover. The smooth rear deck conceals a roomy luggage compartment. Solidly braced, the five-passenger Mercury Club

Convertible body is as practical and convenient in service as it is distinctive in appearance.

FAR AHEAD of its first-year popularity records, the 1940 Mercury 8 continues to win the confidence of experienced motorists. In size, in roominess, in power, in comfort and luxury, the Mercury is everything a big, fine car should be . . . with one important addition: extraordinary ECONOMY of operation. (Owners report up to 20 miles per gallon of gas!) Have you seen the five distinguished body types? Arrange for a personal try-out—the Mercury has a way on the road that speaks volumes.

The Engine Does It All. Touch a knob on the Mercury instrument panel—and the top goes up or down automatically—easily, smoothly, surely. This automatic action increases the usefulness of the top, makes the Mercury Club Convertible a thoroughly practical car to own.

A Roof for Five. Top covers front and rear seats—room for five in comfort—*inside*. Upholstery in Saddle Brown or Antique Finish Red leather. Top in tan or black with red piping. Modern instrument panel and interior fittings in blue-and-silver tones. Eight beautiful body colors.

Built by the Ford Motor Company—distributed by Mercury, Lincoln-Zephyr and Ford dealers

Mercury 8

1

2

1. Filling the vast price gap between Ford and Lincoln-Zephyr, the new-for-1939 Mercury proved instantly successful. Despite styling similarities, not a single outer body panel was shared with Ford. Just $1018 bought the sport convertible coupe. Its 239-cid L-head V-8 developed 95 horsepower, sufficient to make a Merc one of the quickest cars on the road. Mercury started off with hydraulic brakes—new to Ford products. Taillights were visible from the side. **2-3.** The club convertible coupe gained a vacuum-powered top for 1940. Topping the line was a $1212 convertible sedan, but only 1083 were sold and it lasted only one year. New features included a column-mounted gearshift and sealed beam headlights. Mercury issued 9741 convertible coupes, up from 7102 in '39.

3

1

2

3

1. Mercury wheelbases grew by two inches for 1941, to 118. The DeLuxe convertible coupe sold for $1100. Note the lack of quarter windows, which several rival ragtops now included. 2. Car prices rose sharply after World War II ended, and Mercury was no exception. By 1947, a convertible commanded $2002—nearly double the 1939 figure. Since 1942, the flathead V-8 had produced 100 horsepower. Accessory spotlights and foglights decorated many a Merc. 3. Mercury issued a mere 205 Sportsman convertibles in 1946. The cars were trimmed in white ash and mahogany, and, at $2209 each, were the most expensive Mercurys— nearly $500 higher than a steel-bodied ragtop and $200 above Ford's version. More than 6000 regular Mercury convertibles rolled off to dealerships.

1-2. Despite use of the same wheelbase as 1946–48 models, the next-generation Mercury looked nothing like its predecessor. Young buyers, in particular, appreciated the reworked model's vibrant, sinewy lines. In fact, the curvaceous, Lincoln-related new Merc—often hopped-up and customized—quickly became a symbol of freedom for a generation of car-crazed young Americans. By 1950, when 8341 were built, the convertible cost $2412. Mercury's 255-cid V-8 made 110 horsepower; many buyers paid $97 extra for overdrive. Conventional springing replaced the traditional transverse-leaf setup. Note the shapely add-on skirts. **3.** Mercurys appealed not only to youngsters but to families. Desi Arnaz and Lucille Ball drove a yellow Merc ragtop in the popular film, *The Long, Long Trailer*, prompting an untold number of Americans to yearn for a similar vehicle. In 1953, the Monterey convertible listed for $2390. **4.** Restyling for 1952 altered appearance dramatically. Mercury's flathead V-8 still displaced 255 cubic inches but now made 125 horsepower. Only 5261 ragtops were built, as overall output fell sharply. Ford and Mercury shared bodyshells, but Mercs weighed some 250 pounds more.

1

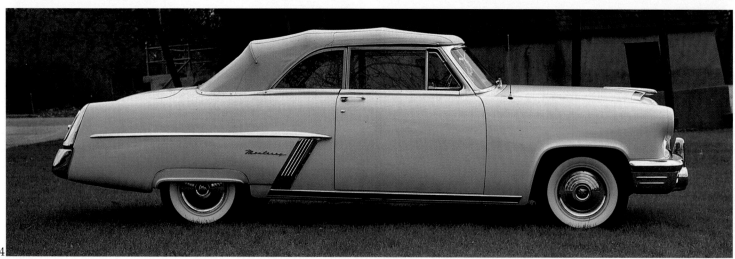

2

3

4

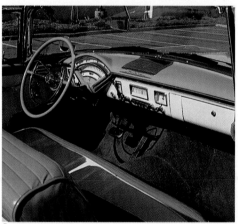

1. Some hot rodders shunned the reworked 1955 Mercury, but production set a record. A total of 10,668 Montclair ragtops were made, starting at $2712. A year earlier, the old flathead engine had given way to a modern overhead-valve V-8. In '55, the V-8 grew to 292 cubic inches and 188 or 198 horsepower. 2. In upscale models, including the '55 Montclair, upholstery often matched or complemented the body color. 3. Mercury had twin convertibles in 1956. The Custom version, shown with spinner hubcaps, skirts, and spotlights, sold for $2712 instead of the $2900 charged for a Montclair. All Mercs had a new 312-cid V-8. This ragtop's body has been "flo-toned" with white. 4. Mercury styling approached its pinnacle in 1957, but this Montclair with a factory continental spare was out-gadgeted by the short-lived Turnpike Cruiser. 5. Pushbuttons controlled the automatic transmission mated to the '57 Montclair's 255-bhp, 312-cid V-8 (or optional 368-cid) engine.

1

2

3

1. In 1957–58 Mercury called its convertibles "phaetons." Only 844 of these '58 Montclairs rolled off the line, each with a standard 383-cid engine. Mercury's optional 430-cid V-8 could deliver up to 400 horsepower. 2. TV's Ed Sullivan touted the 1959 Mercury as the biggest ever, but sales failed to recover after the '58 recession. Only 1257 Park Lane convertibles were built, each holding a 345-horsepower, 430-cid V-8. 3. Dimensions and prices fell for 1961, when the open Monterey—Mercury's sole convertible—went for $3128. The biggest engine now displaced 390 cubic inches. 4. In 1960, the Monterey convertible outsold its Park Lane mate by a four-to-one ratio.

4

1

2

4

3

5

1. Anyone who wanted bucket seats in a full-size Mercury was in luck in mid-1962, when the Monterey S-55 debuted. **2.** Only 1315 Monterey S-55 convertibles were produced during '62, against 5489 plain Monterey Customs, which cost $516 less. **3.** An expanded 1964 lineup brought back the Park Lane as luxury leader, with a 390- or 427-cid V-8. **4.** Renamed Caliente a year earlier, the bucket-seat 1965 Comet convertible could have six cylinders or a small V-8. The 289-cid V-8 was standard in Cyclones. **5.** Full-size models came in Monterey (including bucket-seat S-55) and Park Lane dress for 1967. In that unenlightened era, ads touted Mercury as "the man's car."

1. Station wagons wore woodgrain paneling, but a convertible? Yes, in 1968, Park Lane buyers could order the "yacht" planking option. Only 1112 open Park Lanes were built, and few were "woodies." This car is fully loaded, boasting power vent windows, eight-way power seat, factory air, wire wheel covers, and Select-Shift Merc-O-Matic for the optional 428-cid V-8.
2. Introduced as a coupe for 1967, with hidden headlights, Mercury's Cougar grew in size and added a convertible. The luxury XR-7 cost $213 more than a base Cougar. 3. A 1969 Cougar convertible served as pace car at the Michigan International Speedway. Top engine was a 428-cid V-8, though a 351 was standard. 4. Cougar sales slipped in 1970, when only 1977 XR-7 convertibles were built, and not many more base-model ragtops.

1

2

1. In its third generation, the Cougar grew longer and bulkier, adopting a wider track. The '71 XR-7 convertible cost $3877 and sold just as well as the cheaper model. 2. The Cougar convertible's finale came in 1973, when XR-7 editions easily outsold base models. Federally ordered front bumpers made Cougars longer yet. 3. After going without a ragtop for close to two decades, Mercury dealers got a tiny Capri by 1991. The XR2 held a turbocharged four that produced 132 horsepower. 4. Built by Ford of Australia, Capris bore no kinship to open Mercurys of the past—not with front-drive and a 1.6-liter engine. 5. Capris showed little change for 1993. Sales never managed to take off and the car was gone after 1994.

3

4

5

NASH
and RAMBLER

Nash was among the first makes to issue a convertible body style. Cabriolets debuted in 1928 in the Special and Standard series, priced in the mid-range $2500 neighborhood. At the time, Nash models—which featured classic upright styling—captured better than 3½ percent of the market.

Nashes of the early Thirties were lovely—even sumptuous—machines, with a medley of tempting features. Twin Ignition, for one, meant a single distributor but two of everything else in the system: spark plugs, points, condenser, coil. Top Nashes held overhead-valve eight-cylinder engines, but convertibles also came with six cylinders.

Rumble-seat cabriolets and convertible sedans faded away as Nash cars adopted more streamlined shapes for 1934. The next two years delivered slick Aero-form styling with pontoon fenders and rounded edges but no convertibles at all.

A 3/5-passenger cabriolet appeared in 1937, in three different forms: low-budget Lafayette 400 plus the plush Ambassador Six or Eight. Nash merged with the Kelvinator appliance company this year, bringing not only an infusion of fiscal strength but a new and powerful president, George Mason.

Fashionable restyling for 1939 included a slim vertical grille and flush headlights. Topping the line was the big Ambassador, on a 125-inch wheelbase.

Nash adopted unibody construction for its 1941 models, with a single exception, the Ambassador All-Purpose cabriolet, which stuck with a separate frame.

Only closed cars went to dealers after World War II ended, but an Ambassador Custom cabriolet returned for 1948—the last big Nash convertible. Just a thousand were built, and when Nash turned to "bathtub" styling for '49, no convertible of any kind was in the picture.

Not until 1950, that is, when the compact Rambler debuted—one of the unique open cars of the postwar era, initially offered as a station wagon and a convertible. Instead of the customary fold-back top, Ramblers used a canvas roof that slid rearward on rails—frames fixed in place above the side windows.

Even if they weren't quite as open to the air as some, Rambler ragtops had an undeniable charm all their own. Though rust-prone, the unibodied open Rambler was cute and economical. Priced at a modest $1808, it was also the cheapest ragtop on the market, and 9330 were snapped up in the model's opening season. Rambler convertibles remained on sale through 1954, by which time the price reached a still-moderate $1980.

Nash merged with Hudson in 1954 to form American Motors Corporation.

From then through the end of the Fifties, the only open Nash was the tiny, colorful Metropolitan, built in England with a four-cylinder Austin Engine. In 1959 alone, more than 22,000 Metropolitans went to customers—about one-third of them convertibles.

AMC reskinned the 1953–55 Rambler design in the early 1960s, by now renamed "American" and including a convertible. (See this book's AMC listing for details.)

THIS CLEAN-LINED BEAUTY . . . long, luxurious . . . is best in its class for economy; the Nash Lafayette turning in 23.76 miles a gallon to be a Gilmore-Yosemite Run winner. Yet it streaks from 15 to 50 MPH in 12.9 seconds, *high* gear. The Fourth Speed Forward saves up to 20% on gasoline. 2000 Nash dealers to serve you.

LIVE THE LIFE YOU LOVE . . . touring in "Weather Eye" air, free of dust . . . and stopping and sleeping where you like, in your Nash Convertible Bed. No other car can prepare you for this experience—see and drive a 1940 Nash *now!*

"What Was THAT!"

If you've ever been dazzled by a fleeting blue streak . . . a flash of chrome . . . four spinning wheels . . .

If they disappeared in a puff of dust before you could catch the name—we'll tell you now—it was a 1940 Nash.

And no matter what car you've ever driven—there's no equal to the thrill you'll find at the throttle of a Nash Manifold-Sealed Engine.

It doesn't need a lucky day to get going. Summer or winter, one tap of your toe —and you're off in a breath-taking flash. Surprised? Wait—

Suddenly, you hear a "click" . . . your engine seems to go asleep—yet faster, *faster* . . . the road unreels beneath you.

You're in Nash's Fourth Speed Forward. The power is there. The speed is there. But the sound and fury are gone.

Yet—the real thrill's *still* in the throttle. A car ahead challenges your way. You tap your toe—and your engine leaps into life with a terrific burst of passing power. It's a new Automatic Overtake!

You never felt a car get away so easily . . .

steer so freely . . . cruise so softly. It's Nash's Arrow-Flight ride — and it's exclusive; never anything like it before.

There are Sealed Beam lights in front . . . and, in easy reach, a "Weather Eye" dial to keep air constantly fresh, clean —and warm when you need it.

After fifteen minutes—you'll know why they say, "Once you get your hands on a Nash, you'll never rest 'til you own it."

• • •

It's good for the best 100,000 miles of your life—and then some.

It's backed by resources of $45,000,000, and because we put more into it—you get more *out* of it.

Features like its double-framed chassis . . . 7-bearing crankshaft . . . complete rust-proofing, are yours for longer life and greater resale value.

And the price—is only a few dollars more than a lighter, smaller All-3 car.

So what's holding you back? Just for the sheer fun of it, go for a spin in this new Nash. Call your Nash dealer—now!

You'll be Happier in a NASH

1-2. One of 25 first-series Nash cars issued in 1932, the Model 981 convertible Victoria sedan served as the glamorous member of its five-model group. Rivaling Buick's Series 60 phaeton, the convertible cost $1325. Nash issued nine series this year, with eight engines. Series 980 used a 94-bhp, 240-cid straight eight with Twin Ignition. One-piece bumpers and a mildly vee'd grille were new. Special features included automatic chassis lubrication and a clutch-operated starter. **3-4.** A 125-bhp, 322-cid Twin Ignition Eight powered 1933 Ambassador convertible sedans, which cost $1875 and weighed 4470 pounds. A total of 610 top-of-the-line Ambassadors were built, on 133- and 142-inch wheelbases. Note the Pilot Ray driving lights.

1

2

3

4

1

2

3

4

1. Nash reentered the convertible fold in 1936 with a 400 DeLuxe cabriolet coupe, packing a rumble seat and 90 horsepower. 2. Charles W. Nash looks almost dwarfed by a 1937 Ambassador Eight cabriolet coupe on a 125-inch wheelbase. Convertibles came in all three series: Lafayette 400 and Ambassador Six/Eight, priced from $885 to $1180. Fender skirts added flair to late-Thirties cars. 3. After the war, young athletes would shun Nashes in favor of Fords and Chevys, but this 1938 Ambassador Six cabriolet just might have attracted a cheerleader or two. 4. Each 1940 Nash series included a convertible coupe—Ambassador Six and Eight, and low-priced Lafayette. These couples demonstrate that there's easily room for two more inside a Nash. 5. A cabriolet was one of six 1940 Lafayette body styles. 6. Nash called its 1941 Ambassador Eight an All-Purpose cabriolet. No open '42s were issued. 7. Nash's first postwar convertible arrived for 1948 but lasted only one season.

5

6

7

1

2

1. No other 1951 convertible looked anything like a Nash Rambler Landau, with a fabric top that slid backward along fixed "bridge beam" rails.
2. Rambler gauges sat in a round pod ahead of the driver. Despite their compact dimensions, Ramblers were lavishly equipped, and at $1993, cost a tad more than a Ford ragtop. Standard gear included a Weather Eye Conditioned Air system, deluxe radio, turn signals, and clock. **3.** From the rear, an open Rambler Landau's roll-back top structure resembled a full-length sunroof more than a conventional convertible.

3

1

2

3

1-3. No more domestically built convertibles left AMC factories, but 1954 saw the first Nash Metropolitans—ragtops and hardtops. Built in England on a petite 85-inch wheelbase, Metros used a 1200-cc Austin A-40 engine, rated at 42 horsepower. Note the quarter windows and continental-style spare tire.
4. AMC's minicar became the second best-selling import, its sales total peaking in 1959 at approximately 22,300 units. The colorfully painted Metros by then used a 1500-cc engine that made 52 or 55 horsepower, and added a handy decklid and vent windows.

4

OLDSMOBILE

Known for innovation in the Thirties, then playing a pivotal role in the "horsepower race" of the Fifties, Olds entered the convertible fray in 1929. Its short-lived companion make, named Viking, included a convertible coupe.

After 1933, Oldsmobile pared down its lineup, but with the exception of 1934, a convertible coupe was available in both the six- and eight-cylinder series. Only once did Olds offer a convertible sedan—in 1940–41, as part of the luxury 98 series.

Like other automakers, Oldsmobile fielded facelifted '42 models immediately after World War II. Then, in mid-1948, Olds launched an all-new, modern "Futuramic" 98 series. Convertibles came only in DeLuxe trim, billed as "so modern, so youthful in style [with] a hint of the future in its many automatic features." Close to 17,000 ragtops went on sale in '48, in three series, making Oldsmobile Number Three in convertible production.

Each series again had a convertible in 1949, but the six-cylinder Futuramic 76 paled behind the startling new "Rocket" V-8 engine that powered 88s and 98s. The longer-wheelbase 98 sold best, but Rocket 88s, blending a lighter body with the new V-8's zest, quickly established a reputation as the cars to beat for swift road action.

Sixes disappeared after 1950, and a Super 88 joined the 88 and 98 for '51. The 303.7-cid V-8 earned a power boost for 1952, rising further in '53. Like Buick and Cadillac, Oldsmobile offered a special-edition convertible, named Fiesta. Only 458 were produced.

Ninety-Eight convertibles adopted a Starfire badge in 1954. (By then, the "98" designation was typically spelled out.) In the mid-Fifties, Olds offered two convertibles a year: Super 88 and Starfire Ninety-Eight, joined by a "regular" 88 in '57.

The Starfire nameplate disappeared during 1958–60, then returned in mid-1961 on an 88-based personal-luxury series designed to rival Ford's Thunderbird. In 1962, Olds had a convertible in nearly every series: compact F-85 and Cutlass, Dynamic 88 and Starfire, and luxury-liner Ninety-Eight.

During 1964, Oldsmobile refocused on performance, launching a 4-4-2 option package. The numerals initially stood for a four-speed gearbox, four-barrel carburetor, and dual exhaust. A 400-cid V-8 replaced the initial 330-cid engine in 1965. The next year, nearly 22,000 buyers plunked down extra bucks to transform a mid-size Olds into a 4-4-2.

By 1970, a mighty 455-cid V-8 took charge of 4-4-2 performance. Two years later, the 4-4-2 was demoted to an option package, and the final mid-size Cutlass ragtops rolled toward dealerships.

Big Oldsmobile convertibles had been issued each year, but 1970 saw the last open Ninety-Eights. By 1973, the only convertible left was the Delta 88 Royale, a 4298-pounder that accounted for 7088 sales. Output sunk to 3716 Royales in '74, but shot up to 21,038 in 1975. Why? Because that was the announced "finale" season, and Oldsmobile took full advantage in promoting their sale.

In the Nineties, Oldsmobile was back with a far different breed of convertible, based on the front-drive Cutlass Supreme and wearing a "targa bar." Sales never took off, and the ragtop departed after 1995, but it served as a modest reminder of the era when Oldsmobile was a major player in motoring excitement.

Tomorrow's Classic

Oldsmobile Ninety-Eight Convertible, A General Motors Product

Hydra-Matic Super Drive, GM Hydraulic Steering, Autronic-Eye, white sidewall tires (when available) optional at extra cost. Equipment, accessories, and trim illustrated subject to change without notice.

This is the climax of the "classic" idea in motor cars! This is the car that brings the "ultra-long look" to the convertible field—the Oldsmobile *Ninety-Eight!* Here, for you, is a new measure of grace and glamor and low-poised beauty in an automobile. Interiors are the richest in Oldsmobile history—luxurious long-wearing leather over deep-foam rubber, sparkling new trim, beautiful new color combinations! And above all, this is a "Rocket" Engine car —powered by Oldsmobile's famous new 160-horsepower engine! Paired with new Hydra-Matic Super Drive*, the "Rocket" brings you a thrilling new kind of smooth, effortless action. GM Hydraulic Steering* and the exciting new Autronic-Eye* make driving easier and safer than ever! Drive *tomorrow's classic*—the Oldsmobile *Ninety-Eight* Convertible Coupé! It's *yours today* at your Oldsmobile dealer's!

"ROCKET"

OLDSMOBILE

Ninety-Eight

1

1. Each subseries of the 1930 Oldsmobile F-30 line included a convertible roadster: Standard, Special, or DeLuxe Six, with a 62-horsepower F-head engine. Note the touring trunk. Oldsmobiles could have wood or steel wheels. **2.** Olds's upscale Viking companion, priced higher than a regular Olds, was marketed only in 1929–30, and included a convertible coupe in a three-model lineup. Oldsmobiles used six-cylinder engines, but Vikings ran with straight eights rated at 81 horsepower. **3.** The 252-cid inline engine in a 1937 Olds Eight convertible coupe made 110 horsepower. Only 728 were produced. **4.** Billed as "spirited, youthful," the six-cylinder Oldsmobile convertible in 1937 sold for $965 and sold twice as fast as the Eight. **5.** Headlights moved atop fenders for 1938, but convertibles still had rumble seats. Once again, the open Olds came as a Six or Eight.

2

3

4

5

1

2

3

1. Two of Oldsmobile's three series for 1939 included a convertible coupe, topped by this Series 80. Only 472 were made, but the six-cylinder Series 70 saw 1714 ragtops. **2.** The best-selling 1941 Olds convertible coupe was the Series 66, with a 238-cid L-head six. This car has Hydra-Matic, which debuted on '40 models. Note this year's inboard headlights and the lack of quarter windows. **3.** A Series 68 convertible coupe with a 257-cid straight-eight cost $1089 in 1941. Fender skirts cost $14 extra but gave Oldsmobiles a cleaner look. **4.** Only in 1940–41 did Oldsmobile offer a convertible sedan, dubbed "phaeton." Only 119 copies of this '41 Series 98 Custom Cruiser Eight went on sale.

4

1. A 303.7-cid V-8 went into both new "Futuramic" Oldsmobiles for '49: the trim 88 and stretched-out 98 (shown). A total of 12,602 Series 98 ragtops went on sale but only 5434 of the 88s—and 5338 sixes. By now, most Oldsmobiles had Hydra-Matic. **2.** Oldsmobile launched the "Futuramic" look with the Series 98 convertible during 1948, to replace the older-styled Dynamic 98. All but two of Oldsmobile's six series included a ragtop that year. Note the tiny round parking lights. **3.** Spirited motion was the hallmark of the 1950 Oldsmobile 88, which wrapped a Chevrolet-based body around its vigorous V-8 engine. Convertibles were a little slower than coupes, due to extra weight. **4.** Sold only in 1953, the limited-edition Fiesta featured leather upholstery, a wraparound "Panoramic" windshield, and 10 more horses than a regular Ninety-Eight.

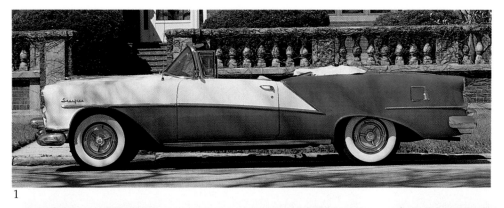

1. Starfire script and pointy body trim decorated each 1954 Oldsmobile Ninety-Eight convertible, now sporting a Panoramic windshield. Shoppers snapped up 6800 Starfires, upholstered in saddle-stitched leather with a passel of power accessories. 2. Softer bodyside trim marked the 1955 Starfire Ninety-Eight, and the 324-cid V-8 delivered as much as 202 horsepower via four-barrel carburetion. 3. Engines gained even more potency for 1956, when a Super 88 convertible sold for $3031. 4. The 1956 Starfire Ninety-Eight convertible cost $709 more than a Super 88 but sold almost as well—more than 18,000 in all.

1. All three "Golden Rocket" series included a convertible for 1957, topped by the Starfire Ninety-Eight. The Rocket V-8 grew to 371 cubic inches and 277 horsepower. In addition to a continental spare, this gaudily trimmed Starfire has power seats, windows, and antenna. **2.** Oldsmobiles never adopted towering fins, but by 1958 their bodies were slathered with chrome. Super 88 was the mid-priced series, with a 305-bhp V-8. **3.** Despite a price $771 higher than a comparable Super 88, the lengthier 1959 Ninety-Eight sold better.

1

2

3

1. Though similar in appearance to 1959 models, the 1960 Oldsmobiles wore all-new sheetmetal below the beltline. Convertibles continued to sell strongly, led by 12,271 Dynamic 88s. **2.** A 1960 Super 88 stickered at $308 more than the Dynamic 88, but $770 below the Ninety-Eight. The 394-cid V-8 yielded 315 horsepower. **3.** Big Oldsmobiles gained new sculpted bodies with pointy rear ends for 1961. Ninety-Eight convertible sales slumped quite a bit, to 3804 cars. **4.** A completely different Starfire emerged for 1961, solely as a convertible. Fully loaded, Starfires featured fancy interiors with air conditioning and leather upholstery, plus a slightly tweaked version of the Super 88's 394-cid V-8 engine. Listing at $4647, it was the most expensive Oldsmobile by far.

4

1

2

3

4

1. Purists doubtlessly disagreed with the phrasing, but Oldsmobile called the 1963 Starfire convertible a "full-size sports car." Oldsmobile's hottest 394-cid V-8, whipping up 345 horsepower, went into every bucket-seat-and-console Starfire—which still cost more than the big Ninety-Eight. **2.** Rebodied for 1965, full-size Oldsmobiles gained a few curves. A 425-cid V-8 rated at 360 horsepower went into Ninety-Eights for the first time. **3.** An all-new Starfire debuted for 1965, with a tapering roofline and roomier interior. Side moldings ended in functional dual exhaust outlets for the 370-bhp, 425-cid Super Rocket V-8 engine. A four-speed gearbox became available for the first time, as did the new Turbo Hydra-Matic transmission that promised "almost unbelievably smooth, instantaneous response." **4.** Smallest and top-selling of the five 1965 Oldsmobile ragtops was the $2983 Cutlass, on a 115-inch wheelbase with a standard 330-cid V-8.

1

2

3

4

1. A full-size Dynamic 88 ragtop with a 425-cid V-8 cost $3404 in 1966. Olds continued to offer a broad convertible line, from mid-size Cutlass to big Dynamic and Delta 88s, to the biggest-of-all Ninety-Eight. **2.** By 1967, Oldsmobile was sending a half-dozen convertibles to market. Largest and most expensive was the Ninety-Eight, starting at $4498. **3.** A high-performance offshoot of the Cutlass, the 4-4-2 came in five models for 1966, including a $3118 convertible. Just one engine was available: a 350-horsepower, 400-cid V-8. Standard gear included heavy-duty springs/shocks, a louvered hood, and bucket seats. Olds called the 4-4-2 an "anti-boredom bundle on rubber." **4.** Full-size Oldsmobiles grew bigger yet in 1969. The $3590 Delta 88 used a 455-cid V-8.

2

1. Still a separate series in 1969, the 4-4-2 convertible packed a 400-cid V-8, rated at 325 to 360 horsepower. Rebodied like its Cutlass parent on a shorter wheelbase for 1968, the 4-4-2 got a new split grille this year. 2. Engine displacement for the 4-4-2 grew to 455 cubic inches in 1970. Only 2933 convertibles left the line, priced at $3567. 3. Horsepower ratings of the 4-4-2 eased downward in 1971, as the muscle-car era began to fade. Ragtop sales skidded by more than half. 4. Hurst and Oldsmobile joined forces to create special variants of the 4-4-2, which was reduced to an option group for '72. 5. By 1973, only one Olds convertible remained: the $4442 Delta 88.

3

4

5

1

2

3

4

1. Convertibles were about to leave the Oldsmobile scene in 1975, but more than 21,000 soft-top fans put down $5200 to grab one of the final full-size Delta 88s. A 350-cid V-8 was standard, but the massive 455 was an option. **2.** As the Nineties emerged, convertible enthusiasts had a new choice: an Olds, of all things. Introduced late in the previous model year, the 1991 Cutlass Supreme ragtop had a "structural top bar" supposedly to help compensate for lost rigidity when the top was snipped off a coupe. Not cheap at $20,995, front-drive Supremes used a 3.1-liter V-6 that yielded 140 horsepower. **3.** A stronger 3.4-liter V-6 was available for the 1993 Cutlass Supreme convertible, issuing a helpful 200 horsepower. **4.** By 1995, its final season, the open Cutlass Supreme stickered at $25,460.

PACKARD

Convertibles came early to the Packard stable, further cementing that marque's illustrious reputation as a builder of superlative American motorcars "for a discriminating clientele." Each of the three chassis marketed in 1928 could hold convertible coachwork: Eight, Custom Eight, and the less-costly six, which was about to disappear. The most prestigious Packards could top $6000, but a '29 convertible coupe, bodied by Dietrich, might be obtained for $3350.

Packard moved a bit downscale with the Light Eight of 1932, and further yet with the One Twenty, introduced in 1935. The latter's name signified a 120-horsepower straight eight engine and 120-inch wheelbase. Those mid-priced models—and the subsequent six-cylinder One Ten—helped save the faltering company but soon began to eat away at Packard's luxury image. Lower-cost lines included convertible coupes, but so did the Twin Six (V-12) series that debuted in 1932. Convertible sedans, too, were sprinkled throughout Packard's broad range of models, including the One Twenty.

Twelve-cylinder Packards were gone by 1940, when Howard "Dutch" Darrin created some of the most striking models of all. Issued in tiny quantities in 1940–41 only, the dramatically opulent Darrin convertible Victorias and sedans brought custom-bodied craftwork to a crescendo.

At the lower end of the scale, even six-cylinder prewar Packards came in convertible dress. A new Clipper "envelope-style" body emerged just before World War II, but restyled ragtops had to wait until the war ended.

To satisfy the clamor for modern convertibles, Packard released a Super Eight in 1948, six months ahead of other body styles. Custom Eight convertibles, far more lavishly fitted, rode a longer wheelbase. With those two on the block, Packard became the country's biggest producer of luxury convertibles, a title that soon would be snatched away by Cadillac. Adapted from the Clipper body, the '48s added flow-through fenders and 200 extra pounds, prompting snickers about the "pregnant elephant" shape. All Packards now contained straight eight engines, the six having been consigned to the dust heap after 1947.

That postwar profile continued until 1951, when Packards earned a whole new look: a squared-off but appealing notchback design that bore no resemblance to the old elephants. Convertibles were part of the picture but only in the standard-wheelbase 250 series.

To refurbish its long-lost reputation for sumptuous luxury, Packard needed a stunner—and got one in 1953. Designer Richard Teague created the Caribbean, a limited-edition soft top with memorable open-wheel styling, a strengthened straight eight engine, and a hefty sticker price. Even at $5210, though, a Caribbean cost considerably less than that year's Cadillac Eldorado.

Caribbeans continued into 1954–56, moving to a longer wheelbase and becoming Packard's sole convertible in the latter two seasons. Meanwhile, Packard had officially purchased the Studebaker company in 1954, but before long it was evident that Stude would dominate, and Packard was to play second fiddle. Thus, the last "real" Packards were the '56 models, and the final 1957–58 Packards were essentially fancied-up Studebakers—with no convertibles of any kind. With that move, one more great name in auto manufacturing—and convertible chronology—ignominiously faded into history.

Designed by the Wizards of "Ah's!"

WATCH the envious glances—hear the enthusiastic "Oh's!" and "Ah's!"—when this sleek, glossy Packard convertible glides up to the curb!

For here is a gloriously new and daring concept of what a convertible should really be—and every breath-taking inch of it is Packard precision-built.

Its husky, newly-engineered chassis (*100 pounds heavier than that of the sedan*) gives this convertible a safety, a rigidity, an in-the-slot stability and quietness no other

Packard convertible has ever matched.

The new straight-eight Packard engine—whether it's the 145-h.p. Super or the 160-h.p. Custom—gives you a brilliance of performance and a whispering surge of reserve power such as you've never known.

In its rich interior appointments there's dazzling beauty, and a touch of magic, too. Press a button and the top lowers or raises. Another button moves the front seat forward or backward! And *all four* windows have magic push-button control!

Don't deny yourself the thrill of seeing the glamor car of '48 at your Packard dealer's!

ASK THE MAN WHO OWNS ONE

THE NEW

PACKARD

*Out of this world . . .
into your* ♥ *heart!*

The Packard Station Sedan is an entirely *new kind* of car. Here's sedan luxury for six—with the easy-loading, carry-all utility of a station wagon. All steel, finished in Northern Birch.

PACKARD

1. Dietrich did the coachwork for this 1931 Custom Eight Victoria, with a 384-cid straight eight and four-speed gearbox. No frugal flyer at $5175, the 4418-pound car seated four. Note the mirrors, seldom-seen options. 2. Packard slid down the price scale with the 1932 Light Eight, which sold for $1940 as a coupe-roadster. About 1060 were made, with a 320-cid engine. 3. Launched a year earlier, the 1933 Packard Twelve, wearing Dietrich Victoria coachwork, weighed 5175 pounds. The 445-cid V-12 made 160 horsepower. 4. The Packard Eight coupe-roadster rode a 136-inch wheelbase in 1934 and cost $2580. 5. A close-coupled '34 Victoria Twelve bodied by Dietrich on the 147-inch chassis cost a daunting $6080.

1

2

3

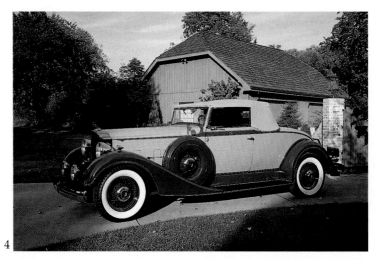

4

5

1

2

4

3

1. Packard Twelves conveyed a decidedly streamlined air by 1934. Series 1108, on the long 147-inch wheelbase, was available as a Dietrich-bodied convertible-runabout, for $6100. **2.** In its second season, the 1936 One Twenty switched from "suicide" to front-hinged doors. A convertible coupe like this one paced the Indy 500 race and was presented to the winner. **3.** Extra-cost goodies brightened the appeal of a 1937 One Twenty convertible. Popular from the start, the One Twenty rescued Packard from the ravages of the Depression. **4.** Although the Dietrich firm had failed in 1935, its name was used for this 1937 Model 1507 Victoria Twelve—actually built by Murray Body.

1

2

3

1. Sixteenth Series Packards for 1938 were restyled from the driver's seat forward, with pontoon fenders replacing the sweeping classic look. The convertible Victoria Twelve rode a wheelbase five inches shorter than before but weighed a hefty 5345 pounds and cost $5230. **2.** Wearing skirts, a 1938 Packard Eight convertible (temporarily losing the One Twenty badge) had riveting good looks. It could be driven home for $1365. **3.** Six-cylinder Packards arrived in '37. This handsome 1940 One Ten convertible was one of six body styles.

1

3

1. Dashing is the best way to describe the 1940 Darrin One Eighty Victoria, wearing a rakish soft top and devoid of the usual running boards. Notching of the "suicide" doors was a sporty trademark of the designer, "Dutch" Darrin. Up front, the cars were stock Packard, but Darrin turned them into works of auto art. **2.** Packards clung to traditional vertical grilles in 1941, but a modern-shaped Clipper was on its way. This One Eighty, and its far-cheaper One Sixty counterparts, held a 356-cid straight eight that made 160 bhp. **3.** Headlights eased into the fenders when the One Twenty series was restyled for 1941. A year later, the One Twenty and six-cylinder One Ten were gone.

2

1

2

3

1. Dealers asked $3250 for the 7763 Super Eight convertibles issued in a long 1948 model year and $1045 more for the 1105 Custom Eights—Packard's flagship. Inverted-bathtub styling drew both cheers and jeers, and earned half a dozen design awards. 2. Moving to a conventional body let Packard offer a new Mayfair hardtop as a companion to the expected, if costlier, convertible—both in the 250 series. A 327-cid straight eight engine sent its power to manual shift, overdrive, or Ultramatic. 3. Full wheel cutouts with chromed openings and an airscoop hood made the 1953 Caribbean convertible easy to spot—if not so easy to buy, with a $5210 price tag. Nevertheless, 750 well-heeled shoppers drove one home. 4. Each Caribbean rode Packard's shorter, 122-inch wheelbase and carried a continental-style spare tire. Packard considered the Caribbean its full-size "sports car."

4

1. Caribbeans may have earned the glamour prize in 1953, but a "regular" Packard convertible cost only $3486—a saving of $1724. The standard convertible had twice the production run of the Caribbean. Both ragtops employed Packard's 180-horsepower, 327-cid inline eight engine. 2. Despite its short-wheelbase chassis, the regular 1954 convertible was trimmed rather lavishly, like senior Packards. The top straight eight engine grew to 359 cubic inches and 212 horsepower. 3. Two-tone paint and more conventional rear-wheel cutouts made the 1954 Caribbean a little less dramatic than before but emphasized the car's length. Standard equipment expanded to include power windows and a power seat. 4. Those who liked two-tones a year earlier had an extra "tone" on tap for the 1955 Caribbean. Like other Packards, the Caribbean got a massive facelift, along with a new 352-cid V-8 engine and Torsion-Level suspension.

1

2

3

4

167

PIERCE-ARROW

Identifying a Pierce-Arrow in the Twenties and early Thirties was easy. Nearly every other American automobile had its headlights in separate units, but Pierce's were faired into the fender tops.

Not quite so evident was the meticulous craftsmanship for which Pierce-Arrow had earned a superlative reputation. Pierce and the other two "Ps" (Packard and Peerless) radiated refined luxury, but excellence does not always translate into healthy sales. Begun in 1901, Pierce-Arrow Motor Car Company evolved from a bicycle manufacturer, reaching its zenith in the late teens. Through the Twenties, Pierce-Arrows were highly admired but technically obsolete, and the company stood in frail financial shape. Studebaker acquired Pierce in 1928. Despite having Studebaker's president, Albert R. Erskine, hold an equivalent post at the luxury firm, Pierce-Arrow was to remain independent, with decisions made at its Buffalo, New York, headquarters. Turning from six-cylinder engines to a new eight in 1929 helped to boost Pierce's weakened image. Not only were the new models quicker and sleeker, but the line now included a convertible coupe, along with the expected touring cars, phaetons, and closed body styles.

Two convertible coupes made the 1930 lineup: Model A, on a 144-inch wheelbase, and Model B, riding a 134-inch span. Pierce-Arrow launched two V-12 series for 1932. By then, convertible sedans were available, offered with a 398-cid V-12 engine and a straight eight.

Despite the smooth, silent V-12, a host of technical improvements, and the publicity resulting from speed records, sales dipped to just 2234 cars. Even more serious, the company lost $3 million in 1932. Like other luxury automakers, Pierce-Arrow had underestimated the seriousness of the Depression. By 1933, Pierces came in four series, each comprising at least two convertible bodies. One of these, the extravagant Model 1247, was custom-built by LeBaron.

Roy Faulkner, former president of Auburn, took over as Pierce's sales manager late in 1932. As one of his first moves, Faulkner exhibited a futuristic Silver Arrow sedan at the Chicago and New York auto shows in January 1933. Designed by Phil Wright, that revolutionary concept car attracted plenty of attention but failed to trigger.

Worse yet, Studebaker went bankrupt in spring 1933, and the company's receivers ordered that Pierce-Arrow be sold. A group of Buffalo businessmen paid $1 million for the newly independent firm, hoping to break even if only they could move 3000 cars a year—or earn a tidy profit if the total hit 4000.

Streamlined 1934 restyling borrowed a few curves from the Silver Arrow show car but customers failed to respond. Sales dipped just slightly that year, but the 1935 total fell by half.

A voguish redesign for 1936, which included dazzling two-passenger convertible roadster-coupes on massive wheelbases, brought a brief promise of recovery. But those hopes soon were dashed. Production halted in 1937, after just 192 cars (plus three dozen '38 models) were issued. Right to the end, Pierce-Arrow's lineup included open roadster-coupes and convertible sedans—rare birds indeed, then and now.

Four-passenger Sport Phaeton of Group A . . . $3750 at Buffalo

ENDLESS ARE THE EXAMPLES OF PIERCE-ARROW SURVIVAL VALUE

A sidelight on Pierce-Arrow character is the almost affectionate regard in which this car is held by so many of America's most representative families. Some of the most enviable Pierce-Arrow service records have been made within these distinguished circles. . . . Neither great dependability, nor exceptional performance, could alone win preference for the same Pierce-Arrow year after year. But both qualities combined, and enhanced by real patri-

cian character, have won a great unchanging loyalty to America's finest motor car . . . To the graceful beauty, the loveliness of appointment and courtly conveyance which have always been Pierce-Arrow, is now added the new luxury of Free Wheeling— the most important automotive development of the past decade.

TWENTY-NINE NEW MODELS . . . WITH FREE WHEELING from $2685 to $6400 at Buffalo. (Custom-built Models up to $10,000)

MR. JOSEPH E. WIDENER, *nationally-known financier and sportsman, has owned the Pierce-Arrow shown in the photograph since 1920.*

PIERCE-ARROW

1

3

4

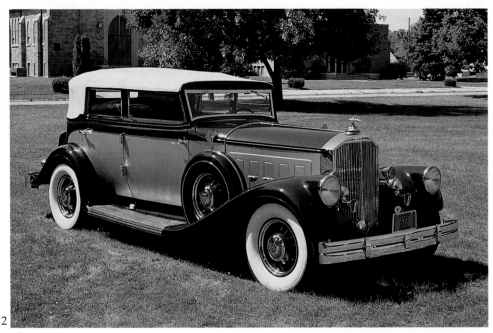

2

1. In 1931, the mid-level Series 42 included a $3650 convertible coupe on a massive 142-inch wheelbase, tipping the scales at 4698 pounds. Pierce-Arrow's sales slid to 4522 cars in 1931—down 46 percent in two years. Headlights that were integrated into fender tops made Pierces easy to identify. **2.** Pierce-Arrows came in four series for 1933, including this Model 1242 convertible sedan on a 137-inch wheelbase, with newly skirted fenders and a $4250 price. Bored to 462 cubic inches, its V-12 engine produced 175 horsepower. The four-door convertible weighed a hefty 5438 pounds. Calendar-year production dropped to 1776 cars, including 118 in this series. **3.** Radiator caps on classic automobiles were works of art, including Pierce-Arrow's delicate, stylized archer. **4.** Running a 3.50-inch bore and 5.00-inch stroke, the 385-cid straight eight engine used in 1931 models developed 132 horsepower.

1

2

3   4

1. The LeBaron coachbuilding firm created a five-passenger Salon body for this 1933 Pierce-Arrow Model 1247 convertible sedan. This long-wheelbase (147-inch) masterwork weighed 5466 pounds and cost $5700 ($6100 in partitioned form). Only 143 examples of Model 1247 went on sale, in all body styles. 2. Dashboards held handsome round gauges in a central panel. Power brakes were standard in 1933. 3-4. "Pierce 12" inscriptions in the trunk emblem and hubcaps left no doubt as to the type of engine used in this 1933 model. With new hydraulic lifters, the 462-cid V-12 made 175 horsepower, but Model 1236 used a smaller V-12. Pierce-Arrow also continued to offer eight-cylinder automobiles.

PLYMOUTH

Chrysler Corporation's lowest-priced make issued its first convertible in 1930. A year later, Plymouth was a rising rival to Ford and Chevrolet, and was first with "Floating Power," meaning that engine mounts were lined with heavy rubber. Simple? Sure, but that innovation helped Plymouth reach Number Three in industry output, a position it held for the next quarter-century.

Standard and Deluxe lines included convertibles in 1932. Model-year 1933 brought a switch from four- to six-cylinder engines. Sales fell in 1934, when convertible coupes came only in the DeLuxe series. By 1937, Plymouth's ragtop output amounted to only 3110 cars. Just when other automakers were about to abandon convertible sedans—if they hadn't already—Plymouth turned one loose in the market. That soft-topped four-door appeared in 1939, but sold only 387 copies and failed to reach a second season. Two-door convertibles, on the other hand, had something entirely new: a vacuum-powered top. This was significant when even luxury motorcars had manual tops.

In the years just before and after World War II, Plymouth issued a convertible only in its top line. Unlike their higher-priced cousins in the Chrysler hierarchy, Plymouth's droptops lacked quarter windows.

From its 1949 redesign through the Fifties, Plymouth never approached Ford or Chevy in convertible output. Each year, only the most costly series included a soft-top body style—Cranbrook for 1951–53, then Belvedere through '58.

Best known as a reliable family car, the low-budget make just couldn't shake its conservative, if not stodgy, image. Even the shapely, colorful restyle of 1955 failed to send convertible sales soaring. Ditto the dramatic reworking for '57.

Plymouth marketing staffers didn't help much, at all. When the hot Fury debuted in 1956, for instance, only a hardtop coupe went on sale—no Fury convertible until '59. Finally, in that year, Plymouth sent twin convertibles to dealerships, finishing the season with its highest sales since 1950. Fast and flashy, the short-lived Sport Fury could have as much as 305 horsepower from an optional 361-cid Golden Commando V-8 engine.

Unibody construction for 1960 was followed two years later by an unwise downsizing that sent sales into the gutter. After issuing full-size Fury convertibles in 1960–61, the Fury dropped to mid-size dimensions. On the plus side, the Sport Fury was revived in '62. Compact Valiants went topless in 1963.

Through the mid-Sixties, Plymouths, like their Dodge counterparts, could be ordered with muscular V-8 engines, including the fabled, race-oriented Hemi. Mid-size Belvedere and Satellite convertibles for '65 rode the former Fury's mid-size wheelbase. Two years later came the Belvedere GTX—a hardtop coupe and convertible, with standard 440-cid V-8. Plymouth's first-generation Barracuda of 1965–66 lacked a convertible, but that deficiency was remedied in the second-generation design of 1967–69, and also in the final rendition that arrived for 1970. Road Runners joined the ragtop ranks for 1969. By 1970, Plymouth had six convertibles on sale. A year later, the Barracuda and its 'Cuda spinoff were Plymouth's last remaining convertible offerings—until late in the Nineties, that is, the target date for a far different breed of open Plymouth, the slinky neo-hot rod called Prowler.

SEEN IN THE BEST PLACES!

THEY CATCH THE EYE at country clubs and smartest resorts—these beautiful Plymouth "Sportsmen"! They're a new high in smartness...yet *low-priced!*

You'll be thrilled with Plymouth's new High-Torque Performance and new power-gearing. You shift gears less! And you enjoy the luxurious roominess and riding comfort of a 117-inch wheelbase!

In the new Convertible Coupe, you get red leather seat cushions, white sidewall tires and the famous power-operated top —*all standard equipment.* PLYMOUTH DIVISION OF CHRYSLER CORPORATION.

PLYMOUTH'S NEW SPECIAL DE LUXE 4-PASSENGER COUPE (below)—a low-priced car of great distinction—is surprisingly roomy. Auxiliary seats can be conveniently folded out of the way. You have a huge luggage compartment in the rear deck. And you get the smart fittings and appointments you might expect to find only in a high-priced car!

THE HANDSOME, ARISTOCRATIC NEW PLYMOUTH STATION WAGON (below) is one of America's most popular town and country cars. Built on the Special De Luxe Plymouth chassis, it offers remarkable roominess, riding smoothness, and handling ease. It is available in natural finish or 2-tone body. Auxiliary seats are quickly removable and interchangeable.

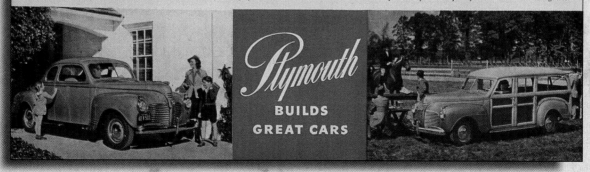

Plymouth

BUILDS
GREAT CARS

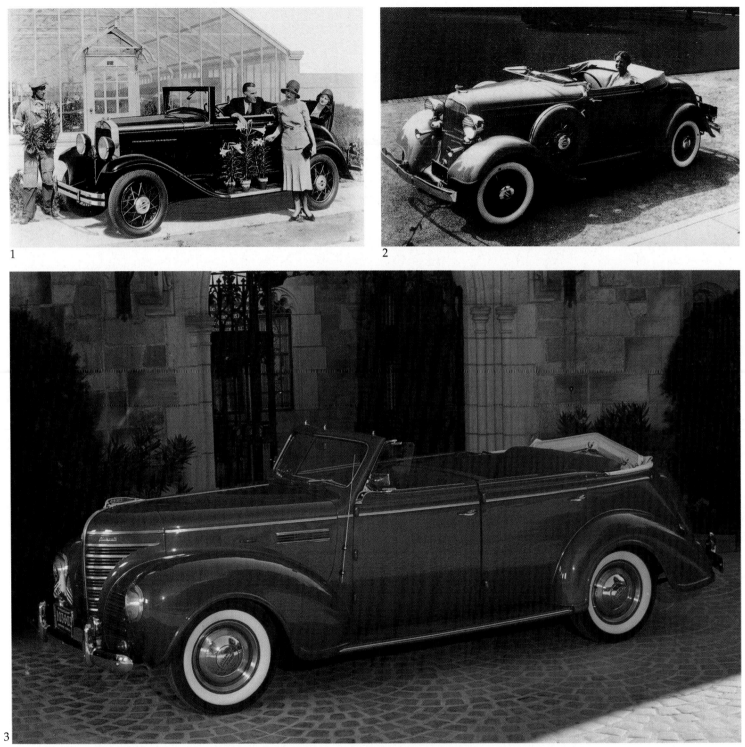

1. Plymouth issued 1272 Model 30-U rumble-seat convertible coupes in 1930–31, the 196-cid four rated at 48 horsepower. **2.** First Lady Eleanor Roosevelt took the wheel of a late '33 PD convertible, its windshield dashingly folded. Plymouth's six-cylinder engine made 70 horsepower. **3.** Only in 1939 did Plymouth offer a convertible sedan—seldom seen, then or now. Hardly cheap at $1150, this was Chrysler's last stab at an open four-door.

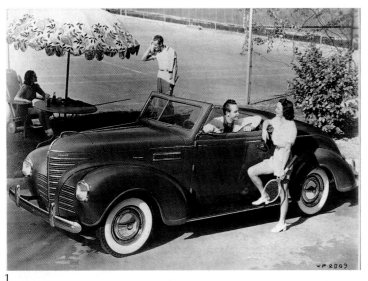

1. Plymouths appealed to budget-minded buyers in 1939, but promotional photos also pictured leisure-time pursuits—logical when the subject vehicle was a jaunty convertible coupe priced at $895. **2.** Young movie star Mickey Rooney eagerly promoted production of the four-millionth Plymouth, a 1941 Special DeLuxe convertible that sold for $1007. **3.** Painted in bright colors, a 1941 convertible belied Plymouth's conservative image.

1

3

2

1. Plymouth claimed ten engineering advances for its 1941 Special DeLuxe convertible, including safety-rim wheels. Customers drove 10,545 ragtops home. Most cars had eliminated running boards earlier, but Plymouths kept them into '41. Rear ends held a trunklid-mounted brake light for the first time. **2.** Only 1.4 percent of Plymouths were convertibles in the early postwar years. In 1948, the dapper Special DeLuxe ragtop sold for $1857. **3.** Raising or lowering the power top on a 1946–48 convertible was no chore.

1

2

1-2. All-new Plymouths failed to arrive until spring 1949 and were boxier than before. A '49 Special DeLuxe convertible cost $1982 (without fender skirts), with 15,240 built. Plymouth's six-cylinder engine, still 217.8 cubic inches, made 97 horsepower. **3.** "Beautifully New" Plymouths for 1950 gained a simpler grille, smooth bumpers, and faired-in taillights. A Special DeLuxe convertible looked spiffy, but output dropped to 12,697 cars. Though stodgy in comparison to curvy Chevrolets and modest in performance against Ford's long-lived V-8, Plymouths attracted practical-minded buyers.

3

1-2. Square corners and flow-through fenders marked the redesigned 1953 Plymouths, which were a tad stubby in profile but had snappy personalities. Just 6301 Cranbrook ragtops went on sale, stickered at $2220; wire wheels and skirts cost extra. Plymouth's aging L-head six delivered 100 horsepower and could be coupled with a Hy-Drive semi-automatic transmission. **3.** Top-of-the-line Plymouths took a Belvedere badge in 1954, led by the $2301 convertible. Exactly 6900 were built. During '54, Plymouth switched to a larger (230-cid), 110 bhp engine and could get the new PowerFlite fully automatic transmission. **4.** Not only did Plymouths get all-new, longer "Forward Look" styling for 1955, they offered optional "Hy-Fire" V-8 engines rated at 241- or 260-cid, and making as much as 177 horsepower. Again heading the line, the open Belvedere cost $2351, with 8473 produced.

1. Plymouths sprouted mild fins for 1956, when the $2478 Belvedere convertible sold 6735 copies. Splashy two-toning gave a youthful image, but the new Fury came only as a hardtop. 2. "Suddenly It's 1960," ads said of the 1957 Plymouths, which were lower, wider, and lovelier, and trailed by sweeping fins. This single-hued Belvedere looks elegant, but many wore flashy Sportone paint. 3. Plymouth launched the '59 Sport Fury to rival Chevy's Impala. This loaded ragtop, holding a 305-horse V-8, went for a lot more than its $3125 base price.

1

3

2

1. As pictured in publicity photos, loftily finned 1960 Plymouths looked even longer than they actually were. A fancy Fury convertible cost $2967, and 7080 were produced, running with a 318-, 361-, or new 383-cid V-8. **2-3.** Lopping off the tailfins gave 1961 Plymouths a fresh profile promoted as "harmony of motion." This Fury sports the distinctive Sportone paint scheme that became available at mid-year. Nearly 7000 ragtop fans signed up for a Fury, which started at $2967, with optional engines as large as 413 cubic inches. **4.** Just 4349 buyers drove home a newly shrunken 1962 Fury convertible. Americans weren't yet ready for mid-sizes, so to help bolster sales, a bucket-seated V-8 Sport Fury, this time packing as many as 420 horses, was revived at mid-year. Only 1516 of those rolled into dealerships.

4

1-2. Styling turned square and conservative in 1963, but Plymouth had a pair of ragtops to entice fun-in-the-sun folks. The $3082 Sport Fury (shown) came only with V-8 power and bucket seats. A tamer Fury ran $178 less. Between the two, Plymouth issued 9057 convertibles. **3.** First offered two years earlier, the 1965 Valiant 200 convertible cost $2437. A fancier Signet went for $124 more. This year's range also included a mid-size Belvedere II and Satellite, and restyled Fury III and Sport Fury—the biggest Plymouths ever. **4.** A full-size 1966 Sport Fury had bucket seats and a standard 318-cid V-8. Buying a Fury III instead saved $177. Engine choices reached to 440-cid.

1

2

1. A standard 440-cid V-8 went into the mid-size 1968 GTX—a Belvedere offshoot launched a year before. Only 1026 were made, starting at $3590. Some had a Street Hemi engine. **2.** Restyling of the Barracuda for '67 added two body styles, including a convertible. This one has the 273-cid V-8, but a 383 went into Formula S Barracudas. Only 4228 ragtops went on sale. **3.** The rarest '68 Barracuda was the convertible, with just 2840 built. The Formula S version (shown) included a tach and heavy-duty suspension, along with a four-barrel, 275-bhp, 340-cid V-8. **4.** Plymouth had hoped to rival Mustang and Camaro with its Barracuda, but '69 volume dipped to 1442 convertibles. A 275-bhp 340-cid V-8 was optional, dubbed 340-S. Striping cost extra.

3

4

1

1. Aiming at twentysomething buyers, Plymouth snipped the top off its Road Runner in 1969. Sales were meager, despite hot V-8 choices. 2. Only 635 open 'Cudas went on sale in 1970. The cars were bigger and bulkier than before, and came in base and Gran Coupe guise. 3. 1970 'Cudas could have a 440-cid V-8, or even the intimidating Hemi. 4. Introduced at the 1993 Detroit Auto Show as a concept car, Plymouth's Prowler eventually headed for production—to the surprise of skeptics. Back-to-basics styling evokes images of Fifties street rods, but technology will be strictly up-to-date.

2

3

4

PONTIAC

No one had devised a true convertible body when the first Pontiacs arrived in 1926. Three years later, the "New Big Six" lineup included a cabriolet. Pontiac's soon-to-expire companion, the Oakland, also offered a convertible in its final seasons.

In 1932, Pontiac convertibles could have either a six or a new 85-horsepower V-8, the latter borrowed from the now-expired Oakland but lasting only one season. Pontiac turned to straight eight engines for 1933, continuing the cabriolet body style. By 1936, convertibles came in three series: Master and DeLuxe Six, and DeLuxe Eight.

Not until 1937 did Pontiac issue convertible sedans and only for two seasons. Convertible coupes continued into the Forties, available as soon as Pontiac resumed production after World War II. By 1948, Pontiac ranked fourth in convertible production, turning out 16,000.

Postwar restyling arrived in 1949, and convertibles were part of the upscale Chieftain series. Pontiacs got a blockier look for '53, with twin convertibles. A year later, the new step-up Star Chief series offered the sole Pontiac convertible.

Like all Pontiacs, Star Chiefs gained Strato-Streak V-8 power for 1955, dropping both the six and the inline eight. A lower-cost Chieftain droptop arrived in 1958, leaving the Star Chief without a convertible. Meanwhile, in mid-1957, that gap was filled by a stunning limited-edition Bonneville.

Semon "Bunkie" Knudsen had recently taken over as general manager, determined to energize Pontiac's staid image. Bonneville was the first result. Comparable to Chevrolet's first Impala, packing a bored-out V-8 with Rochester fuel injection, Bonneville ushered in a nameplate that continues in the Nineties.

Dropped sharply in price for 1958, Bonneville then became a four-model, top-of-the-line "Wide-Track" series. By 1960, nearly as many Bonneville convertibles were sold as Catalinas, despite a $398 price differential. Next year, the Bonneville ragtop topped Catalina's volume by half.

Pontiac ranked second in GM's convertible production throughout the Sixties. After 1967, Pontiac reached Number Two in the entire industry. The early lineup of full-size Catalinas and Bonnevilles was augmented in 1962 by compact open Tempests. Then, during 1964, Pontiac launched the car that virtually jump-started the muscle-car generation: the Tempest GTO, in coupe and convertible dress.

Sporting mid-size dimensions, the GTO firmly established Pontiac's reputation as the make to beat in full-bore performance. Less-vigorous Tempest and LeMans droptops remained available, joined in 1966 by a Catalina-based 2+2 and then, for one season only, a ragtop version of the personal-luxury Grand Prix. Coupe and convertible Firebirds debuted in 1967 but the 1970½ restyle eliminated soft-tops.

By 1971, the muscle-car era was fading, and GTO production began to skid. Catalina and mid-size LeMans convertibles lasted through 1972, but open Bonnevilles were gone after '70. Following a batch of '75 models, even the big Grand Ville droptop was extinct.

Soon after Chevrolet introduced its Cavalier convertible in 1983, Pontiac snipped the roof off some of its Sunbird subcompacts. Firebird convertibles joined during 1991, and the latest Sunfires also are available with fold-down tops.

THE BREATH-TAKING

BONNEVILLE

Famed race driver Pat O'Connor and his lovely wife, Analice

ANOTHER *Pontiac First!*

A SPECIAL LIMITED-EDITION

Sports Convertible

HAND-CRAFTED LUXURY

plus FUEL-INJECTION POWER

Feast your eyes on Pontiac's dream car to end all dream cars—the incomparable Bonneville! Here is the advanced creation that thrilled thousands who saw it at Daytona. Here, in a masterpiece of engineering, Pontiac combines brilliant styling and incredible luxury with the ultimate in modern V-8 performance . . . Fuel-injection Power!

PONTIAC MOTOR DIVISION · GENERAL MOTORS CORPORATION

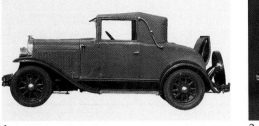

1

2

3

4

1. Pontiac's first convertible arrived in 1929, in the New Big Six series, priced at $845 and painted shadow brown with orange trim. 2. In 1935, the cabriolet cost $775 as a DeLuxe Six or $840 as an Eight. New "Silver Streak" striping would endure through '56. 3. Switching from "suicide" to front-hinged doors in 1936, the DeLuxe Six was one of three cabriolets. 4. Pontiac had a new choice for '37: a $1235 DeLuxe Eight convertible sedan. 5. Like other Eights, the 1937 convertible sedan rode a new, longer 122-inch wheelbase. Its engine also grew, now making 100 bhp. 6. Again in 1938, the DeLuxe Eight line included two- and four-door convertibles.

5

6

1. By 1939, rumble seats were history. Pontiac convertibles had an internal back seat, so all occupants were protected when the weather took a bad turn. This DeLuxe Eight cost $1046, with a 100-horsepower, 249-cid engine. Buying the Six instead saved just $53. 2. Pontiac convertibles wore a DeLuxe Torpedo badge in 1941, and were again available with six- or eight-cylinder power. Foglights, spotlights, and fender skirts added to a ragtop's allure. 3. Prices shot skyward after the war, when a 1946 Torpedo convertible cost at least $1631 ($1658 with the straight eight). In '47, ragtops came with base or DeLuxe trim, but only the DeLuxe edition hung on. 4. Copywriters claimed that "the racy appeal of the 1948 Pontiac convertible [created] the appearance of increased length and lowered center of gravity." Hydra-Matic Drive joined the option list, at $185. Four out of five Eights had it; in the meantime, six-cylinder Pontiacs were losing favor fast. This year's Pontiacs were the first to flaunt "Silver Streak" badges.

1. A glamorous 1950 Chieftain DeLuxe Eight cost $2190, but a lower-cost six rode the same wheelbase. 2. By '52, all but seven percent of buyers chose an Eight. At $2518, the Chieftain DeLuxe Eight convertible cost less than a wagon. 3. Pontiacs added a little style in 1953. Fender skirts gave a clean stance to the Chieftain DeLuxe Eight. 4. For 1954, the new Star Chiefs sported an extended deck. All four models had a straight eight. 5. Sporty wire wheel covers boosted the $2691 base price of a 1955 Star Chief—now boasting a 287-cid V-8.

1

2

3

4

5

1. American Pontiacs abandoned six-cylinder engines for 1955, but Canadians could get a new Laurentian convertible with a 261-cid Chevrolet truck six. Riding Chevrolet's 115-inch wheelbase, the ragtop was available with an optional 162-horsepower Chevy V-8 instead. 2. In 1956, the extended-length Star Chief was once again Pontiac's sole convertible. The 327-cid V-8 could have twin four-barrel carbs and 10:1 compression for 285 horsepower. Chromed skirts were a rakish touch. 3. Buyers liked their Star Chiefs fully loaded. This skirted '57 ragtop has special-order colors and a continental spare, plus a Tri-Power upgrade of the enlarged, 347-cid V-8. Pontiac's "trademark" Silver Streaks were gone.
4. Pontiac went all-out to eradicate its stodgy image with the $5782 Bonneville. Only 630 were built in late 1957, with a fuel-injected 370-cid V-8.

1. Bonneville convertibles dipped to just $3586 in 1959, when 3096 were produced—against 9144 of the new hardtop coupes. Its 370-cid V-8 could have fuel injection or Tri-Power carburetion.
2. Pontiacs adopted a split grille and went "Wide-Track" for 1959, expanding the distance between wheels for better stability. With Tri-Power, the Bonneville's 389-cid V-8 made up to 345 horsepower. A total of 11,426 ragtops were built, starting at $3478 ($398 more than a Catalina).
3. Base engine for the little-changed 1960 Bonneville with Hydra-Matic was a 303-bhp, 389-cid V-8. Stickshift engines had less power. **4.** All Pontiacs, including the Bonneville, shrunk considerably as part of the 1961 redesign. Reduced weight boosted performance, especially from the optional 348-horsepower, 389-cid Tri-Power engine.

1

2

3

4

1. Starting in 1962, the innovative four-cylinder Tempest, featuring a flexible driveshaft, could be ordered in convertible form, either Deluxe or LeMans (shown). 2. LeMans became a separate Tempest series in 1963, when 15,957 ragtops were sold. This LeMans has the optional 326-cid V-8. 3. Not much time was needed for the 1964 GTO to become an American legend. GTOs came with quick steering, stiff shocks, and dual exhausts. The 389-cid V-8 had available Tri-Power, a four-speed, and tach, and other "go" goodies could be added. Most GTOs were hardtops, but 6644 buyers took a ragtop. 4. A Bonneville-based Club de Mer toured the 1964 show-car circuit. 5. This Canadian-built 1965 Acadian Beaumont holds a 283-cid V-8. 6. Stacked headlights and a hood scoop marked 1965 GTOs. The Goat's top V-8 cranked out 360 horses.

5

6

1

2

3

4

1. Bonnevilles gained a little length in the 1965 redesign, but kept the standard 389-cid V-8. Shoppers must have liked the look, for 21,050 ragtops found homes. 2. Now a separate series, the 1966 GTO gained new sheetmetal with bulging fenders. Output set a record, including 12,798 convertibles that started at $3082. 3. Not much was new on the 1966 Bonneville, but droptop output dipped to 16,299. 4. Starting in 1964, Pontiac offered a 2+2 option for its full-size Catalina—including a 421-cid V-8. The 1966 version (shown) cost $3602, versus $3298 for a 2+2 hardtop. 5. Only in 1967 did the Grand Prix series include a convertible, priced $264 above the hardtop.

5

1

2

3

4

5

1. Bonneville grew to a five-model series in 1968, when the convertible started at $3800. A 340-bhp, 400-cid V-8 was standard. 2. A 400-cid V-8 could be installed in Firebirds from the start. Only 16,960 ragtops went on sale for 1968, the model's second season, against 90,152 hardtop coupes. 3. Mid-size two-doors adopted a new A-body and 112-inch wheelbase for 1968. One of six Pontiac convertibles, the '69 LeMans cost $3064. 4. Pontiac revamped the Bonneville for 1967, installing a heavy bumper/grille, boring the standard V-8 to 400-cid, and adding a 428-cid option. Droptops accounted for 8902 sales. 5. Ads called the 1967 GTO "The Great One." The V-8 grew to 400 cubic inches, rated at 335 bhp.

1

2

3

5

4

6

1. Six-cylinder Firebirds earned a following of their own. A Sprint package for 1968 convertibles included a 215-bhp upgrade of the overhead-cam engine. Rally gauges with a hood-mounted tach added $84. **2.** Firebirds got new sheetmetal for 1969. This one has the six-cylinder Sprint option, with 230 horsepower and a four-speed. **3.** Pontiac had four convertibles in 1970, including the $3604 Catalina with a standard 400-cid V-8 or optional 455. **4.** Production of GTO convertibles fell to only 661 cars in 1971—plus 17 wicked "Judge" ragtops. **5.** Grand Ville was a new name for full-size Pontiacs in 1971, with a 455-cid V-8 and a $4706 sticker. **6.** By 1973, Grand Ville was the only ragtop left, going to 4447 customers.

1

2

3

4

5

1. Initially sold only in LE trim, the open Sunbird was available in GT trim in 1986, complete with a turbo engine. 2. After a slow start, Sunbird convertible production grew to 13,197 in 1990. 3. For the first time in a dozen years, rear-drive Firebirds went topless in mid-1991. 4. Redesigned a year earlier, the 1996 Sunfire lineup included an SE convertible. 5. Restyled as an early '93 model, Firebird lacked a convertible until 1994. In addition to base V-6 and Formula V-8 ragtops (shown), Pontiac offered a striking white/blue 25th anniversary Trans Am.

SHELBY

Legendary driver Carroll Shelby retired from racing in 1960, but wasn't about to give up on automobiles. Deciding to build some stark, quick road cars, he began in 1962 with Shelby-Cobras. These were created by plopping a Ford V-8 engine into a lightweight Ace chassis, obtained from A.C. Cars in England. Small-block 287-cid V-8s were installed initially, but Shelby graduated to mammoth 427s that packed as much as 425 horsepower. On the road or around the track, Cobras rank among the hairiest thrill machines ever. Therefore, the 1000-plus cars built are now expensive collectors' items.

Not quite so costly, but no less popular, are the Shelby-Mustang GTs built from 1965 to '69. Produced in limited numbers, early race-inspired examples were named GT-350. Work was accomplished at the Shelby-American facility in Los Angeles.

Shelby-American workers began with a white-bodied, blue-striped Mustang fastback coupe, containing the Hi-Performance rendition of the 289-cid V-8, rated at 271 horsepower. Adding a Hi-Rise manifold, bigger carburetor, free-flow exhaust, and other items boosted output to 306 horsepower at 6000 rpm. Additional gear included Koni adjustable shocks, specially cast 15-inch alloy wheels, metallic braking surfaces, and quick-ratio steering. Hertz Rent-A-Car actually ordered 936 special GT-350H models in 1966, with Select-Shift Cruise-O-Matic instead of the usual four-speed gearbox.

A year later, Shelby took the newly enlarged Mustang and tucked in a new 428-cid V-8 engine for the new GT-500. Both models wore a more aggressive fiberglass nose, plus a clipped Kamm tail with a prominent spoiler. Interiors added a thick roll bar with built-in inertia-reel seatbelts.

Only a half-dozen prototype convertibles were built in 1966, but open Shelby-Mustangs made the production list for 1968. By then, the cars were manufactured at Ford rather than Shelby, and thus were neither as stark nor as harsh as the originals. Interiors now held a stock Mustang dashboard, for instance, and optional air conditioning, power steering, and automatic transmission could be installed. Convertibles cost about $100 more than fastbacks, which remained available.

In mid-1968, the GT-500 transformed into a GT-500KR ("King of the Road"), now holding the latest 428-cid Cobra Jet engine that breathed through a huge Holley carburetor. Shelby-Mustangs issued in 1969 were closer yet to showroom-stock Mustangs, as restyled that year. Shelby versions got a large loop bumper/grille and a host of scoops and ducts, as well as reflective tape stripes. GT-350 editions dropped to Ford's new 351-cid "Cleveland" V-8. No longer dubbed "King," the GT-500 still carried a Cobra-Jet engine, rated at a nominal 335 horsepower—but actually putting out quite a few more horses. Just 3150 of the '69 Shelbys went on sale, with 636 leftovers renumbered as 1970 models. Existing and forthcoming government regulations, plus spiraling insurance rates—due in part to a staggering GT accident rate—played roles in the Shelby's demise. So did the hot, more affordable new showroom Mustangs, such as the Mach 1 and Boss 302. All told, about 1100 GT-500 and fewer than 700 GT-350 convertibles were issued, including the final 1970 examples.

Carroll Shelby has gone and done it!

Convertible types, rejoice! He's built Shelby COBRA GT performance, handling, style and safety into a Mustang *convertible* complete with the best-looking roll bar in the business. If you

don't flip your lid over this, you just don't flip (unless his Mustang-based Cobra GT 2 + 2 fastback gets to you). □ Both styles are available in GT 350 or GT 500 versions. The GT 350 boasts 302 cubic inches of Ford V-8 performance with an optional Cobra supercharger for added zip. The GT 500 really delivers with your choice of two great V-8's . . . 428 cubic inches are standard. A new 427 engine is the ultimate performance option. □ All the Le Mans-winning handling and safety features are better than ever for 1968. They're wrapped up in a fresh new luxury package. And the Mustang base means an exciting price. □ Any questions? Your Shelby Cobra dealer has some great answers!

Shelby COBRA GT 350/500
POWER BY FORD

1

2

1. After modifying only Mustang fastbacks in 1965–67, Shelby turned to high-performance convertibles. The GT-500 carried a standard 390-cid V-8, but many examples, including this ragtop, held a 428-cid V-8 rated at 360 horsepower. Note the twin hood scoops and original-style 10-spoke wheels. 2. Just 402 Shelby GT-500 convertibles were produced for 1968, plus 404 GT-350s with a 302-cid V-8. 3. Priced at $4439 (versus $2712 for a basic Mustang fastback), the 1968 GT-500 wore a Kamm-style tail and standard roll bar.

3

1

2

3

1-3. Output from the 428-cid Cobra-Jet V-8 engine installed in the 1969 Shelby GT-500 was estimated at 400 horsepower. A four-speed gearbox sent all that strength to the back wheels. Only 335 GT-500 convertibles were built (not counting leftovers sold in 1970), along with 194 GT-350 ragtops that used a 290-horsepower, 351-cid V-8 engine. Shelbys were far from cheap ($5027 for this year's GT-500), but the driving experience they delivered was well worth the entry fee.

STUDEBAKER

No American car's history reaches back farther than that of the Studebaker, which traces its lineage to carriages and covered wagons built in 1852. Studebaker also turned out to be an early convertible contender.

During the winter of 1927–28, Studebaker announced availability of a rumble-seat cabriolet in the Commander Regal and President State series. Stylish bodywork blended with a powerful engine to produce a memorable machine.

By the summer of 1928, Studebaker had three four-seat convertibles in its revised lineup, including the new Dictator Royal. A two-passenger convertible coupe also was offered in the Erskine line, on a 108-inch wheelbase—one of the smallest around. The Commander Six convertible cabriolet of 1929 held a 74-horsepower, 248-cid six and cost $1495.

Studebaker entered the Thirties with a broad lineup of vehicles—and the prospect of financial collapse. By 1933, Erskine and Rockne, Stude's secondary makes, had failed. Pierce-Arrow took over the company, which resulted not in glory but receivership. Studebaker survived the merger far better than Pierce, and officials went to work on developing Studebakers that would sell.

The three-pronged 1934 lineup included a Dictator, Commander, and President Eight, each split into subseries. That gave Studebaker an even half-dozen convertibles: standard and Regal variants in each main line.

Not a single convertible was offered in 1936–37. Then came a convertible sedan, of all things, in all three series. That expensive and rarely seen body style survived into 1939, albeit only in the Commander and President lines, after which no open cars were issued until 1947.

Ads issued shortly after World War II noted that Studebaker was "first by far with a postwar car." And in those heady days for the industry, a convertible was definitely part of the plan. Not only did the Commander line include a ragtop; so did the shorter-wheelbase Champion, a series that had debuted in 1939 in closed form only.

Studebakers adopted a "bullet" nose for 1950–51, then a straight-across grille for '52. Meanwhile, a V-8 engine went into Commanders, while Champions stuck with the small L-head six.

Raymond Loewy's design team turned out an eye-catching coupe in the European mode for 1953, but the avant-garde design never included a convertible. Prototypes were attempted, but production never happened, and so the luscious coupes—including their 1956–64 Hawk successors—hit American roads with no convertible body style.

Studebaker, in fact, was without any kind of ragtop from 1953 to 1958. Then, the compact new Lark arrived on the scene, styled by Duncan McRae and ready to go topless a year after its 1959 debut. Perky and practical, the six-cylinder or V-8 Lark gave the financially faltering company a reprieve.

The last American-built Studebakers—and the final convertibles—rolled off the line at South Bend, Indiana, late in 1963, for the 1964 model year. Ragtop volume plunged to 703 units. Production then moved to Hamilton, Ontario, for two final seasons, but no ragtops made the cut. After 1966, the Studebaker name graced no more cars.

Studebaker Commander convertible

Studebaker's the buy word

for thrift that lasts and style that thrills

Here's the brilliant performance you want in a new car—the flattering smartness—the solid money's worth!

Here's a fabulously fine new 1949 line of pacemaking postwar Studebakers—low-swung, flight-streamed new sedans, coupes and convertibles—new visions of loveliness inside and outside—the most value-packed automobiles that a moderate investment ever bought!

Here's a new kind of operating economy that's a pleasant surprise in these times—amazing savings not only on gas and oil but also on repairs.

Don't wait—stop in at a Studebaker dealer's and see these newest versions of the cars that changed the face of motoring. Your first look is sure to take you a long step toward proudly driving a thrilling new Studebaker of your own.

White sidewall tires, wheel trim rings or discs, available on all models at extra cost.

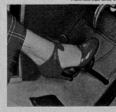

You're flattered by the luxury of refreshingly different decorator fabrics. Pictured is the interior of Studebaker's long-wheelbase Land Cruiser sedan with nylon upholstery superbly tailored over foam-rubber seat cushions.

You use amazingly little gas even on long trips in a postwar Studebaker. Yes, whether on the open road, or in stop-and-go city driving, you can always count on a Studebaker engine to give brilliant, low-cost performance.

Your brakes rarely need servicing —they automatically adjust themselves to lining wear—an exclusive feature of all postwar Studebaker cars. You have the firm brake pedal feel of a new car after months of driving.

Craftsmanship you can trust—Men of conscience as well as competence, many of them members of father-and-son teams, build Studebaker cars to the very highest standards of quality. Studebaker Corp'n, South Bend 27, Indiana, U.S.A.

1

1. Although Studebaker was building fine automobiles in the early Thirties, crisis was looming, though you wouldn't know it from the long list of models. For 1931, seven different series and five engines went on sale, topped by the magnificent President Eights, now recognized by the Classic Car Club of America as full Classics. Like other Presidents, this Series 80 Four-Season convertible roadster, priced at $1900, had a 337-cid straight eight rated at 122 horsepower. Roll-up windows gave convertible convenience, but the car had a roadster's spirit, heightened by a fold-down windshield. New styling included ovoid headlights and fender-mounted parking lights. Note the auxiliary trunk, wind wings, and large driving lights. 2. Even 1932's least-expensive Studebaker series, the 55 Six, included a convertible sedan. Tiny back windows were common, doing little for visibility. Priced at $985, the four-door carried a 230-cid engine rated at 80 horsepower. Convertible sedans also came in Dictator, Commander, and President Eight model designations.

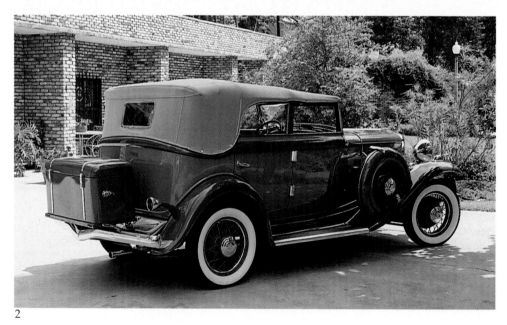

2

1

1. In 1935, Studebaker still called its open two-doors "roadsters." A 107-bhp, 250-cid engine powered this Commander Eight, offered in base or Regal trim. Convertibles also came in the Dictator Six and President Eight series. 2. A bewildering selection of 1934 body styles included the mid-level Commander Eight convertible roadster, with rumble seat, "suicide" doors, and 103-horse engine. 3. After several years without ragtops, Studebaker added a pair when it underwent a linewide restyle after the war. This 1947 Champion Regal DeLuxe sold for $1902. A heavier Commander, with a bigger engine, brought $2236.

2

3

1

2

1. Some called Studebaker's postwar styling sensational. Other Americans made wisecracks and turned to Big Three rivals, with their familiar carryover designs. The 1948 Commander convertible, dubbed Regal DeLuxe and riding a 119-inch wheelbase, wore a $2431 price tag and contained a 226-cid L-head six-cylinder engine delivering 94 horsepower. Champion ragtops rode a wheelbase seven inches shorter, weighed 555 pounds less, and started at just $2060. The Champ's L-head six measured 169.6 cubic inches, and lasted long enough to power the first Larks in 1959–60. **2.** Studebaker chairman Harold S. Vance posed behind the wheel of a 1952 Commander convertible, which paced the annual Indy 500 race. A year earlier, Commanders had dumped the big six-cylinder engine, in favor of an overhead-valve 232.6-cid V-8 that made 120 horsepower. Shoppers could get a Champion ragtop for $275 less than the Commander's $2548 list price.

1

2

3

1. A breezy little convertible, launched in 1960, added zest to the personality of Studebaker's compact Lark. The Regal-trimmed ragtop could have either an L-head six, evolved from the old Champion, or a peppy V-8. 2. Like other Larks, the 1960 Regal VIII convertible rode a 108.5-inch wheelbase. With V-8 power, the sticker read $2756, but taking a six saved $135. 3. With a 180- or 195-bhp V-8 underhood, the 1960 Lark performed passionately. Most convertibles had a V-8, and overdrive transmissions were popular. 4. What better way to see the sights than in a 1960 Lark VIII convertible? No other American compact model included a ragtop—yet.

4

1

2

1. A new overhead-valve six-cylinder engine, rated at 112 horsepower, went into the 1961 Lark VI Regal convertible. A 259-cid V-8 also was available, rated at 180 or 195 bhp. 2. Slight stylistic touch-ups marked the 1961 Larks, which started at $2689 with the V-8 engine. By now, Big Three compacts were coming on strong, and would ultimately doom the little Lark. 3. Renamed Daytona a year earlier, the 1963 convertible had a sporty flair with bucket seats. This one has a six and automatic, but a four-speed and two V-8s were available: 259- or 289-cid. "Super Larks" could get optional Avanti R-1 and R-2 engines, rated at 240 or 290 bhp; the latter supercharged.

3

1

3

2

1-2. Through the years, Studebaker had a strong presence in Canada, but this 1963 Daytona looks just like its American counterparts. Quad headlights became standard a year earlier. **3.** Billed as "Different by Design," the 1964 Studebakers got a clever facelift and new sheetmetal that disguised the carryover structure. The Daytona ragtop cost $2670 with six-cylinder power or $2805 with a 180-horsepower V-8. An optional 289-cid V-8 developed 225 bhp or more. A tiny handful of R-3 and R-4 engines, rated at up to 335 horsepower, were installed in a few Studes. **4.** Squared-up taillights adorned the last Daytona convertibles—and final American-built Studebakers.

4

ORPHANS
& UNDERDOGS

By the Thirties, when the roll-up-window convertible began to flower, thousands of automobile manufacturers had already come and gone. Over the next few years, many of the remaining automakers would follow suit.

Crosley was different, starting up after some of the other independents declined. In 1939, the company introduced one of the first serious American minicars—tiny, thrifty, ahead of its time. Two convertibles debuted: a two-passenger coupe and four-seat sedan. Crosleys rode an 80-inch wheelbase and carried a minuscule air-cooled, two-cylinder engine that promised as much as 60 miles per gallon.

Crosley switched to four-cylinder power when production resumed following World War II. Convertible coupes remained in the lineup until the make's demise in 1952. Not quite fully open, convertibles had fixed pillars and roof rails, with a roll-back soft top. Crosley also produced Hotshot and Super Sports roadsters, with side curtains instead of glass.

Franklin was America's only successful builder of air-cooled automobiles in the Twenties. A convertible first appeared in 1928, in the Airman series. The 1930 selection included long-wheelbase, custom-bodied Pirates, as well as convertible coupes in the Six and Transcontinent Six series—each with a supercharged engine. A revived Airman series for 1932 also offered a convertible. So did the Olympic of 1933–34, a badge-engineered variant of the Reo Flying Cloud. By 1935, though, Franklin was history.

Graham-Paige turned to convertibles as soon as the make debuted in 1928, in the Senior Six and Model 835 Eight series. Standard and Special Eight convertible sedans joined in 1930. The most notable Graham convertible was the 1932 Blue Streak Eight, sculpted by Amos Northup and sporting trend-setting skirted fenders. The company was foundering by then but hung on through the Thirties. Supercharged Eight convertible coupes went on sale in 1935–37, but no open versions of the coveted 1938–40 "sharknose" were produced.

Hupmobile also issued the occasional convertible, between 1929 and 1934.

In the early Thirties, **Marmon** ranked with the likes of Cadillac and Packard as a top contender for the luxury motorcar market. Most had eight cylinders, but the splendid Sixteens also could be ordered with soft tops. Marmon expired after 1933.

Moving into the postwar period, Earl "Madman" **Muntz** had made his fortune in the TV business but wanted to build an American sports car. Descended from the two-seaters built by Frank Kurtis, Muntz's posh 1951–54 Jet seated four and proved to be quick and competent.

Reo turned to convertibles in the early Thirties, issuing some of the loveliest examples of the lot—especially the Flying Clouds. In 1936, though, Reo left the car business.

Wide-open Bearcats had given **Stutz** a reputation for excitement long before the true-convertible era. Speedsters and convertible coupes later bore a Stutz badge—mainly in the DV-32 series that debuted in 1931. Superlative styling and innovative engineering weren't enough to keep the company alive after 1936.

What *is* the most modern car?

With motors especially designed to meet the road requirements of today and tomorrow—

With four-speed transmissions of silent and smooth efficiency—

With the "Noback," an entirely new device which automatically prevents undesirable back-rolling on hills—

With worm-drive and consequently low center of gravity, and its unmatched safety—

With a new kind of *de-celeration*, made possible by the mightiest of brakes—

With safety glass, of course, and brilliant speed and comfort supreme—

These two cars cap the very apex of modernism.

And they have easily commanded a prestige and financial resourcefulness that is a truly modern achievement.

Stutz $3395 to $6895, Blackhawk $2345 to $2955, f. o. b. Indianapolis

STUTZ
and
BLACKHAWK

THE SAFEST CAR HAS THE RIGHT TO BE THE FASTEST

1. Crosleys grew in size after the war and switched from two to four cylinders. Their copper-brazed "CoBra" engine made 26.5 horsepower. A convertible coupe was one of three body styles, selling for $949 in 1947. **2.** Crosley launched two models in 1939. The $325 convertible coupe weighed 925 pounds and seated two. A $350 convertible sedan held four. Each held a two-cylinder engine, rated at 13.5 bhp. Spartan they were—including sliding windows—but far cheaper than any other car. Just 2017 were built in the first year. **3.** Even after the war, Crosleys were inexpensive. Production in 1947 included 4005 convertibles. Note the fixed pillars.

1

2

3

1

2

1-2. Famed stylist Ray Dietrich penned 1930 Franklin Pirate four-door convertibles, as part of Series 147 on a 132-inch wheelbase. Either a seven-passenger touring car or a phaeton could be ordered. Priced at $2885, the Pirate tourer weighed 4050 pounds. A convertible option also was available for four-passenger speedsters. Pirates had concave lower-body contours that fully covered the running boards—an idea that most automakers would not try for another decade. Franklin's air-cooled, 274-cid six-cylinder engine developed 95 horsepower, driving a four-speed gearbox. Fabric-covered sidemounts and Trippe lights were distinctive.

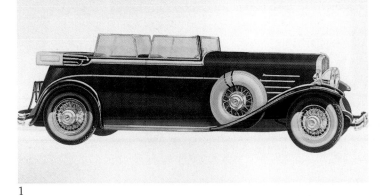

1

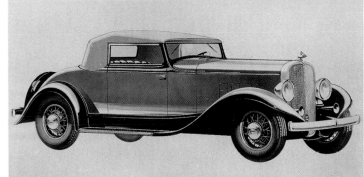

2

1. Described by the Franklin company as "highly streamlined," a five-passenger, dual-cowl phaeton was the second Pirate model, priced identically to the touring car. A Franklin Six convertible coupe cost $2710 in 1930, and the Transcontinent Six went for $2495. **2.** New for 1932, the Franklin Airman Six convertible coupe seated three or five and sold for $2390. Note the "suicide" doors of this 4285-pounder, whose supercharged six developed 100 horsepower. **3.** Custom convertible bodies also went on Franklins, as demonstrated by this sports speedster with coachwork by Dietrich. **4.** Four Graham-Paige series, including this eight-cylinder Model 827, offered a convertible coupe in 1929. **5.** By 1932, the "Paige" suffix was gone. The new, trend-setting Graham "Blue Streak" Eight series grabbed most of the attention, but six-cylinder Grahams also came in convertible coupe form, including this Model 58. Graham's Special Eight series even included a convertible sedan. The slanted, vee'd grille was a surefire attention-getter.

3

4

5

1

1. A second pair of passengers had to climb into the rumble seat to take a joyride in a 1934 Graham Model 67 convertible coupe. Its 245-cid straight eight made 95 horsepower. The supercharged Custom Eight series also included a ragtop.
2. Marmon convertibles might have either a straight-eight or a V-16 in 1932. If a Sixteen was magnificent, the convertible sedan ranked as sheer bliss. Marmon's 491-cid V-16 engine developed 200 horsepower, versus 125 bhp for the Eight. Ads billed the Sixteen as "The World's Most Advanced Car." **3.** Instead of a fold-down top, the 1954 Muntz Jet used a removable hardtop. From 1951 to '54, only about 394 Jets were produced, each selling in the $5500 neighborhood. Celebrities liked the sleek Jets, which came with seatbelts and a padded dash. **4.** Reo listed a wide choice of convertibles in 1933, including this rumble-seated Flying Cloud. Prices started at $1045. A handful of convertibles also appeared in the much-larger Royale series.

2

3

4

1

2

1. Luscious lines and a low windshield distinguished the 1932 Stutz DV-32 cabriolet, shown in "pigeon's blood" hue. Stutz's dual-cam, 322-cid straight eight was a technical marvel good for 161 horsepower. **2-3.** Fabric covered the Weymann-built body of this 1932 Stutz Super Bearcat. Light yet strong, the fabric soaked up noise and was easy to repair. Color was impregnated into lacquer-coated cloth. Super Bearcats seated two and rode a 116-inch wheelbase, while other Stutzes measured 134.5 inches. Price tag for this brand of thrill, in Depression-era dollars, was $5895. A tiny rear window did little for visibility. **4.** Fewer than 50 Stutz cars were built in 1932–33, including this stately '33 DV-32 convertible coupe that sold for $3895. The slanted windshield was new this year on standard bodies, which were built by LeBaron and shipped to Stutz.

3

INDEX

A

Abernethy, Roy, 8
A.C. Cars, 196
American Motors Corp. (AMC),
  8–13, 142
  Ambassador, 8, 11, 12, 13
  Classic, 8, 11
  Custom, 10
  Rambler American, 8, 10, 11, 12
  Rambler Rogue, 13
  Rebel, 8
Arnaz, Desi, 136
Auburn, 14–19, 168
  6-66, 14
  115, 14
  851, 18
  852, 18
  Custom Dual Ratio, 17
  Eight, 18
  Salon Twelve, 17
  Speedster, 14

B

Ball, Lucille, 136
Barrie, Wendy, 73
Buehrig, Gordon, 14, 19
Buick, 20–31
  Centurion, 20, 31
  Century, 20, 22, 23, 26
  Country Club Coupe, 20
  Custom, 30
  Deluxe, 30
  Electra 225, 20, 28, 29, 30, 31
  Invicta, 20, 29
  LeSabre, 20, 28, 29, 31
  Limited, 20, 27
  Master Six, 20
  Model 66C, 22
  Reatta, 20, 31
  Riviera, 20, 31
  Roadmaster, 20, 22, 23, 24, 26, 27
  Series 60, 22
  Series 90, 20
  Skylark, 20, 26, 29, 30, 31
  Special, 20, 22, 24, 29
  Super, 20, 23, 24, 26, 27
  Wildcat, 20, 29, 30
Brunn, 122

C

Cadillac, 32–43
  Allanté, 32, 43

Cadillac (*continued*)
  Biarritz, 32
  Coupe de Ville, 39
  DeVille, 32, 41, 42
  Eldorado, 32, 42, 43
  Eldorado Biarritz, 39, 40, 41
  Fleetwood, 34
  Model 355B, 34
  Sedan de Ville, 39
  Series 61, 35
  Series 62, 32, 36, 37, 39, 40, 41
  Series 75, 32
  Series 90, 35
  Victoria, 32
Carillo, Leo, 61
Carrera Panamericana (Mexican
  Road Race), 122
Cars & Concepts, 58
Chevrolet, 8, 44–57
  Bel Air, 44, 47, 48, 49
  Camaro, 44, 54, 55, 56
  Caprice Classic, 44, 56
  Cavalier, 44
  Chevelle, 44, 52, 54, 55
  Chevy II, 44, 51, 52
  Corvair, 44, 52, 53
  Corvette, 44, 49, 50, 51, 54, 55, 56
  Fleetmaster, 46
  Impala, 8, 44, 49, 50, 51, 52, 53, 55
  Independence, 46
  Special DeLuxe, 46
  Styleline DeLuxe, 44, 47
  Two-Ten, 48
Chicago Auto Show (1933), 168
Chrysler, 8, 58–69, 70, 78, 172
  300, 58, 65, 66
  300E, 63
  300G, 64
  Airstream, 58, 60
  Imperial 80, 58, 60, 63, 64, 66
  LeBaron, 67, 68, 69
  Model 72, 58
  Newport, 58, 66
  New Yorker, 58, 61, 62, 63, 64
  Sebring, 58, 69
  Series 62, 64
  TC by Maserati, 58, 68
  Town & Country, 58, 61, 62, 66,
    67
  Windsor, 58, 61, 62, 63, 70
Classic Car Club of America, 202
Cord, 14–19

Cord (*continued*)
  L-29, 14, 15, 16
  810, 14, 19
  812, 14, 19
  Sportsman, 14
Cord, Erret Lobban (E. L.), 14
Crosley, 208, 210
  Hotshot, 208
  Super Sport, 208

D

Darrin, Howard A. "Dutch," 114,
  160, 165
Dean, James, 132
DeSoto, 70–77
  Adventurer, 70, 77
  Airflow, 70, 73
  Airstream, 70, 73
  Custom, 72, 74, 75
  DeLuxe, 74
  "Finer Six," 72
  Firedome, 70, 76, 77
  Fireflite, 70, 76, 77
  Sportsman, 70
Detroit Auto Show (1993), 183
Dietrich, 58, 122, 124, 160, 162, 163,
  212
Dietrich, Raymond, 70, 211
Dodge, 70, 78–89
  400, 58, 78
  600, 89
  Challenger, 78
  Coronet, 78, 82, 83, 84, 87, 88
  Custom, 81
  Custom 880, 78, 86, 87
  Custom Royal, 78, 84
  Dart, 86, 87, 88
  Dart Phoenix, 78, 85
  D series, 80
  Polara, 78, 85, 86
  Royal, 78, 83
  Shadow, 78, 89
  Sportabout, 78, 82
  S series, 80
  Viper, 78
  Wayfarer, 78, 82
Duesenberg, 14–19
  Model J, 14, 16

E

Earhart, Amelia, 108, 110
Edsel, 90–93

Edsel (*continued*)
  Citation, 90, 92
  Corsair, 90, 93
  Pacer, 90, 92, 93
  Ranger, 90, 93
Erskine, Albert R., 168
Essex, 108
  Challenger, 108
  Model KT, 110
  Pacemaker, 108
  Sun Sedan, 110
  Terraplane, 108, 110, 111, 112

F

Faulkner, Roy, 168
Ford, Benson, 99
Ford, Edsel, 90, 122, 125, 132
Ford, Henry, 90
Ford, Henry, II, 90, 99
Ford Motor Company, 94–107. *See
  also* Shelby.
  Custom, 94
  DeLuxe, 97, 98
  Fairlane, 100, 101, 104, 106
  Falcon, 94, 102, 103
  Galaxie 500, 94, 102, 104, 105, 106
  Model A, 96
  Mustang, 94, 103, 105, 106, 107,
    196, 198
  Skyliner, 94, 100
  Sportsman, 94, 98
  Sports Roadster, 94
  Sunliner, 94
  Super DeLuxe, 94, 98
  Thunderbird, 94, 100, 101, 102,
    103, 104
  Torino, 94, 106
  Victoria, 99
Ford, William Clay, 99
Franklin, 208, 212
  Airman, 208, 212
  Olympic, 208
  Pirate, 208, 211, 212
  Six, 208, 212
  Transcontinent Six, 208, 212
Frazer, Joseph W., 114

G

Graham-Paige, 114, 208
  Blue Streak Eight, 208, 212
  Custom Eight, 213
  Model 58, 212

Graham-Paige (*continued*)
Model 67, 213
Model 827, 212
Model 835 Eight, 208
Senior Six, 208
Special Eight, 212
Gregorie, Bob, 122

H
Hertz Rent-A-Car, 196
Hudson, 8, 108–118, 142
Commodore Six, 112
Custom Eight, 111
DeLuxe Eight, 111
Eight, 108
Greater Eight, 108
Hollywood, 108
Hornet, 108, 113
Landau, 110
Metropolitan, 108
Model 20, 112
Six, 108
Step-down, 108, 113
Super Six, 112
Super Wasp, 12, 108, 113
Hupmobile, 208

I
Iacocca, Lee, 58
Indianapolis 500
1935, 96
1948, 46
1951, 62
1952, 204
1953, 99
1954, 78, 84
1956, 70
1963, 65
1967, 53
1968, 106
1971, 78
1987, 67

K
Kaiser-Frazer, 114–117
Frazer Manhattan, 114, 116
Kaiser Custom, 114
Kaiser Deluxe, 114
Kaiser Special, 114
Kaiser Virginian, 116
Kaiser, Henry J., 114
Kelvinator, 142
Knudsen, Semon "Bunkie," 184
Kurtis, Frank, 208

L
Lady Astor, 110
LaSalle, 118–121
Series 50, 121
Series 303, 120
Series 328, 120
Series 340, 120
Series 345B, 120
Leamy, Alan, 14
LeBaron, 58, 122–125, 168, 171, 214
Lewis, Jerry, 83
Lincoln, 122–131

Lincoln (*continued*)
Capri, 122, 129
Continental, 122, 125, 126, 127, 130, 131
Cosmopolitan, 122, 128
KB Series, 122
Premiere, 122, 129
Series K, 122, 124, 125
Zephyr, 122, 124, 125, 126, 127
Loewy, Raymond, 200
Long, Long Trailer, The, 136

M
Marmon, 208
Eight, 213
Sixteen, 213
Martin, Dean, 83
Mason, George, 142
McCahill, Tom, 99
McRae, Duncan, 200
Mechanix Illustrated, 99
Mercury, 132–141
Caliente, 132, 139
Capri, 132, 141
Comet, 132, 139
Convertible Cruiser, 132
Cougar, 132, 140, 141
Custom, 132, 137
Cyclone, 139
DeLuxe, 135
Marquis, 132
Montclair, 132, 137, 138
Montego, 132
Monterey, 132, 136, 138, 139
Park Lane, 132, 138, 139, 140
Sportsman, 132, 135
Turnpike Cruiser, 132, 137
Michigan International Speedway, 140
Miller, Harry, 14
Moon motorcar, 14
Motorama, 32
Muntz, Earl "Madman," 208
Muntz Jet, 208, 213
Murphy Body company, 110
Murray Body, 163

N
Nash, 8, 108, 142–147
Ambassador, 142, 144, 145
400 DeLuxe, 145
Lafayette, 142, 145
Metropolitan, 8, 147
Model 981, 144
Rambler, 146
Special, 142
Standard, 142
Nash, Charles W., 145
New York Auto Show
1927, 122
1933, 168
NHRA Winternational, 86
Northup, Amos, 208

O
Oakland, 184
Oldsmobile, 148–159

Oldsmobile (*continued*)
Cutlass, 148, 156, 157, 158, 159
Delta 88 Royale, 148, 157, 158, 159
Dynamic 88, 148, 155, 157
Dynamic 98, 152
Eight, 150
F-30, 150
F-85, 148
Fiesta, 148, 152
Futuramic 876, 148
Ninety-Eight, 148, 153, 156, 157
Series 66, 151
Series 68, 151
Series 70, 151
Series 80, 151
Series 88, 152
Series 98, 148, 151, 152
Six, 150
Starfire, 148, 154, 156
Super 88, 153, 154

P
Packard, 160–167
Caribbean, 160, 166, 167
Clipper, 160, 165
Custom Eight, 160, 162, 166
Eight, 160, 164
Light Eight, 160, 162
Mayfair, 166
One Eighty, 165
One Sixty, 165
One Ten, 160, 164, 165
One Twenty, 160, 163, 164, 165
Six, 160
Super Eight, 160, 166
Twelve, 162, 163, 164
Twin Six, 160
Pierce-Arrow, 168–171, 200
Model A, 168
Model B, 168
Model 1236, 171
Model 1242, 170
Model 1247, 168, 171
Series 42, 170
Silver Arrow, 168
Pininfarina, 32
Plymouth, 70, 182–183
Barracuda, 172, 182, 183
Belvedere, 172, 178, 179, 182
Belvedere II, 181
Cranbrook, 172, 178
DeLuxe, 172
Fury, 179, 180, 181
Fury III, 181
Model 30-U, 174
Prowler, 172, 183
Road Runner, 172, 183
Satellite, 172, 181
Signet, 181
Special DeLuxe, 175, 176, 177
Sport Fury, 172, 179, 180, 181
Standard, 172
Valiant, 172, 181
Pontiac, 184–195
Acadian Beaumont, 191
Bonneville, 184, 189, 190, 192, 193

Pontiac (*continued*)
Catalina, 184, 190, 192, 194
Chieftain, 184, 188
Club de Mer, 191
DeLuxe Eight, 184, 186, 187, 188
DeLuxe Six, 184, 186, 187
DeLuxe Torpedo, 187
Firebird, 184, 193, 194, 195
Grand Prix, 192
Grand Ville, 184, 194
Laurentian, 189
LeMans, 184, 191, 193
Master, 184
New Big Six series, 186
Star Chief, 184, 188, 189
Sunbird, 184, 195
Sunfire, 184, 195
Tempest, 184, 191

R
Rambler American, 142. *See also* Nash.
Renault, 8
Alliance, 8, 13
Rebel Without a Cause, 132
Reo, 208, 213
Flying Cloud, 208, 213
Royale, 213
Rickenbacker, Eddie, 96
Romney, George, 8
Roosevelt, Eleanor, 174

S
Shelby, 196–199
GT-350, 198, 199
GT-500, 198, 199
Mustang, 196, 198
Shelby-Cobra, 196
Shelby-American, 196
Shelby, Carroll, 105, 196
Studebaker, 160, 168, 200–207
Champion, 200, 203, 204
Commander, 200, 202, 203, 204
Daytona, 206, 207
Dictator, 200, 202, 203
Erskine, 200
Hawk, 200
Lark, 200, 205, 206
President Eight, 200, 202, 203
President State, 200
Rockne, 200
Stutz, 208
Bearcat, 208
DV-32, 214
Super Bearcat, 214
Stewart, James, 73

T
Teague, Richard, 160

V
Vance, Harold S., 204
Viking, 148, 150

W
Widman, John, 114
Wright, Phil, 168